COIT TOWER,
SAN FRANCISCO

The COIT
MEMORIAL
TOWER
Erected
in
1933

The decoration of
the interior in Fresco
was authorized as a
PUBLIC WORKS
OF ART PROJECT
and undertaken by the
Artists of San Francisco,
and completed
in
1934

COIT TOWER, SAN FRANCISCO

ITS HISTORY AND ART

MASHA ZAKHEIM JEWETT

COLOR PHOTOGRAPHS BY DON BEATTY

VOLCANO PRESS

SAN FRANCISCO, CALIFORNIA

Library of Congress Cataloging in Publication Data
Jewett, Masha Zakheim, 1931–
Coit Tower, San Francisco, its history and art.
1. Mural painting and decoration, American—California—San
Francisco. 2. Mural painting and decoration—20th century—
California—San Francisco. 3. California in art. 4. Coit Memorial
Tower (San Francisco, Calif.) 5. San Francisco (Calif.)—Towers.
6. Public Works of Art Project. 7. Painters—California—Biography.
I. Beatty, Don, 1934– . II. Title.
ND2638.S26J48   1983   751.7′3′0979461   83-5814
ISBN 0-912078-75-8

Black-and-White Photo Credits
Don Beatty: pp. 2, 3, 10, 12, 13, 14, 29, 32, 48, 53, 54, 58, 63, 64 (top);
University of California, Berkeley, Library of Environmental Design:
p. 25; California Historical Society, San Francisco: pp. 19 (I.W. Taber),
20 (Bradley and Rulofson), 21, 23 (Fred Mae, Mission News
Company), 26 (bottom); Maria Ealand, courtesy of Richard D.
McKinzie: p. 31; Emmy Lou Packard: pp. 34, 35, 36, 60, 61, 62; San
Francisco Public Library: pp. 15, 16, 37, 39, 41, 45 (bottom), 52, 59;
Shirley Triest Papers, Archives of American Art, Smithsonian
Institution: pp. 38, 45 (top)

PRODUCED BY PINWHEEL

BOOK AND COVER DESIGN: HOWARD JACOBSEN / TRIAD

COMPOSITION: TYPE BY DESIGN

PRODUCTION COORDINATION: LEIGH DICKERSON DAVIDSON

PRINTED IN JAPAN BY TOPPAN PRINTING COMPANY, LTD.

Additional copies of this book are available directly from the
publisher. Send $10.00 for each book. Add $1.25 postage and
handling plus 50¢ for each additional book. California residents
please add appropriate sales tax.

VOLCANO PRESS, INC.

330 ELLIS STREET, DEPT. B

SAN FRANCISCO, CALIFORNIA 94102

CONTENTS

ACKNOWLEDGMENTS

For many years, my father, artist Bernard Zakheim, tried to interest me in writing the story of Coit Tower. Why would anyone want to know about that "dated art" I used to wonder. I found the answer to that question when I began to incorporate a survey of the artwork into my San Francisco Arts class at City College of San Francisco. Thanks to Don Jewett, who also suggested a guide to the art at the Tower, the students and I went up to look at, then stayed to enjoy this amazing legacy of the 1930s. Other artists helped me to amplify and expand what are essentially primary source materials. There has been no comprehensive study of what valued informant Dr. Francis V. O'Connor called, when I asked his advice, "your gold mine of New Deal Art in San Francisco." John Langley Howard and his brother Robert were early informants; Shirley Staschen Triest, Edith Hamlin, Ralph Chesse, Tino Moya Kun, Helen Clement Mills, and my father contributed their important reminiscences. Mme Marcelle Labaudt gave freely of her time to identify portraits. Helen Oldfield provided information and a feeling for the *mise en scène* of the 1930s.

A grant from the National Endowment for the Humanities gave me time from teaching to pursue the research. Photographer Don Beatty (assisted by Edward Serrano and Lisa Dunwoody) helped me to "see" vignettes and details that I might otherwise have missed. Paul Yuke, former Business Manager of the San Francisco Recreation and Park Department, was an early and enthusiastic supporter of the project, helping in 1977 to reopen to the public the art sections of Coit Tower, which had been locked up since 1960 because of vandalism.

Once the writing was under way, I received much help from Lewis Ferbrache's Public Works of Art (PWAP) archive, Professor Michael Goodman's expert architectural knowledge, Emmy Lou Packard's documented restoration report and comments, and Rita Carroll's and Elaine Molinari's readings. The assistance of Dr. Belisario Contreras has been invaluable in sharpening the section on the PWAP and providing a national overview. Dr. Julius Comroe was very helpful with the technicalities of writing for publication, and asked the question, "Where are the artists now?" which led to my writing the anecdotal biographies in the appendix. Dr. Paul Karlstrom at the Archives of American Art was an initial reader of my earliest research paper and gave me good advice. Nathan Zakheim provided excellent technical information on the fresco technique and restoration.

Editor Ruth Gottstein asked the "hard questions" whose answers tightened loosely written form and content, and Mary Johnson typed the manuscript very professionally.

In addition, I am grateful to the following people who assisted me in various ways: Elio Benvenuto; Robin F. Burgstahler; Chapin Coit; Katherine Colzani; the late Marion Ellis and the staff at Coit Tower; David Fleishhacker; Gladys Hansen; Judith Lynch; Oddette Mayers; Garnett McCoy; John B. McGloin, S.J.; Tom Malloy; Marjorie Fleishhacker Matthau; John Moylan; Bob Popp; Sheldon Rosenthal; John Dormer Smith; and Martin Snipper.

Also very helpful were the administration and my colleagues at City College of San Francisco, especially Terence Alberigi, Diana Fairchild, Katherine Hondius, and Ronald Pelsinger.

The following institutions have faithfully preserved records that aided my work: Archives of American Art, Smithsonian Institution, San Francisco and Washington, D.C.; California Historical Society; City College of San Francisco Library; Oakland Museum of Art Library; San Francisco Recreation and Park Department; San Francisco Main Library, History Room; and University of California, Berkeley, Library of Environmental Design and Bancroft Library.

A grant from the National Endowment for the Humanities gave me the financial support that made the project possible. City College of San Francisco supplemented this grant and provided much valued secretarial time.

FOREWORD

The publication of Masha Zakheim Jewett's book on Coit Tower is not only timely, but fills a very real need. The timeliness of this volume stems from the fact that this year San Francisco celebrates the fiftieth anniversary of the building of the Tower. More significantly, the murals at Coit Tower, which were a pioneer federal arts project, have esthetically stood the test of time. In recent years there has been a growing interest in both the subject matter of the murals and that unique band of artists who created them in so short a period.

Ms. Jewett brings to her project a unique insight. Her father, Bernard Zakheim, was one of the muralists. Written in a fluid and easily comprehensible style, this work details the origin of the project and the intense political and artistic controversy which the murals generated. It contains fascinating details highlighting the social conditions of the time and the enormous wealth of humor and detail these important works of art contain.

To me, personally, one of the great wonders of the collection is how the art in the main room appears to be the work of a single artist. Because of this unique aspect, the collection attains a far greater significance as an entity.

My wish now is that Ms. Jewett would continue her research and publish a comparable delightful volume on those other great federal art projects in San Francisco, namely, the murals at the San Francisco Zoo, Beach Chalet, and Rincon Annex Post Office.

I trust you the reader will derive as much delight and information from this volume as I did.

Tom Malloy
General Manager, San Francisco Recreation
and Park Department
June 1983

INTRODUCTION

Coit Memorial Tower on Telegraph Hill—native and tourist alike recognize this San Francisco landmark. Both Pioneer Park on the crest of the hill and the Tower top offer some of the finest views available of the Bay Area. And even if there were no views, Coit Tower itself is well worth a visit for its local history and its major artwork.

Over 200,000 visitors each year ride the elevator to the top to view the whole San Francisco Bay Area. Stretched out below them are the downtown highrises, the major hotels of the city, and the two bay bridges leading to the surrounding Bay Area communities in the distance. A plaque installed by the Daughters of the American Revolution commemorates the ship-signalling station that used to stand on the summit of Telegraph Hill.

Funded by money bequeathed to San Francisco by "Firebelle" Lillie Hitchcock Coit in 1929 "to add to the beauty of the city I have always loved," Coit Tower was erected in 1933—in memory of a woman with a purported aversion to towers! Although local lore says that it resembles a fire hose nozzle to commemorate Lillie Coit's association with the Volunteer Fire Department of the last century, its architect, Henry Howard, working in the firm of Arthur Brown, Jr., insisted that he was designing a bold but "simple fluted shaft" without any prototype. In the entranceway are replicated two fluted columns, miniature towers themselves, together with twelve others spaced around the gently bowed square foundation. The grey concrete tower rises 180 feet above a rectangular base

32 feet high with an observation deck near the top offering a 360-degree view through its arched windows.

Through the eastern windows one sees the rebuilt Embarcadero, including the old piers; man-made Treasure Island created for the 1939–40 Golden Gate International Exposition (now a naval base); Yerba Buena Island; the San Francisco–Oakland Bay Bridge; the crowded East Bay communities; and the University of California campus in Berkeley, with its campanile.

One of the less appealing aspects of City Life, V. Arnautoff

Through the southern windows lie the 1898 Ferry Building at the foot of Market Street; freeways; the downtown highrises, among them the Transamerica Pyramid and the fifty-two story world headquarters of the Bank of America.

Southwest is Washington Square, with the spires of Sts. Peter and Paul Church in North Beach; and in the distance, gothic Grace Cathedral.

To the west are the forests of the Army Presidio; the Golden Gate Bridge, with its left arch spanning the brick Civil War–era Fort Point; the dome of the 1915 Panama-Pacific International Exposition; zig-zag Lombard Street; and Ghirardelli Square—formerly a chocolate factory, now a shopping mall.

To the north are more Embarcadero piers, including Pier 39; Alcatraz, Angel, and Belvedere Islands; and the Marin Headlands, including the town of Sausalito.

Inside the base of this monument are 3,691 square feet of murals depicting California life as it appeared to the twenty-six artists and their nineteen assistants (themselves artists) who painted the interior walls in 1934, one year after the Tower was opened to the public. Funded by the Public Works of Art Project (PWAP), this artwork constitutes one of the most innovative pilot federal programs of the New Deal. At the time of their completion, the artworks represented three-quarters of all the frescoes on walls in California.

First Impressions

Most visitors to Coit Tower come initially out of curiosity, attracted by the spectacular view and by the novelty of the Tower and its murals. Once there, however, they discover a "time capsule" of art portraying life in California as the artists perceived it half a century ago. Many are surprised to discover scenes of the social, political, and economic concerns of the 1930s, the time of the Great Depression. Today the viewing public is interested to learn that some artists were censured for portraying scenes that suggested ideologies different from those of the established government, the San Francisco Art Commission, and the press—such as scenes of workers marching during the May Day demonstration or a library reader reaching for a book by Karl Marx.

Among local visitors, possibly a parent or grandparent remembers downtown San Francisco flowing with activity as shown in the mural *City Life*—replete with ambulance, fire truck, and pickpockets! Perhaps an aunt recalls working in a 1934 department store; an older man viewing the *Newsgathering* panel is reminded of how he, too, hawked newspapers on the city streets as a boy; a farmer recalls his old ranching friends picking apricots to set out, halved, to dry lusciously in the sun. These vignettes, and more, preserve the life that existed in California and in hundreds of other communities across the nation in the 1930s.

The parallels between the issues of the 1930s and the economic uncertainties of the 1980s seem very real to the viewing public at Coit Tower. The artists depict a California that is sober with the realities of the Depression but optimistic in the natural abundance of good harvests, rich natural resources and their processing industries, and

California's abundance, M. Albro

Hand power versus hydroelectric power, J.L. Howard

sophisticated urban life—and the wealth that flows from the successful meshing of all the parts, suggesting a hopeful future for San Francisco, for California, and for the United States. Although it was an age of guarded optimism and tentative hope, the artists who decorated this memorial to a lovable, eccentric San Francisco woman left an encouraging pictorial record which, transcending their own time and concerns, shows a segment of history to the generations that have come after them.

PART I:
THE HISTORY

THE CONSTRUCTION OF THE TOWER

LIKE Rome, San Francisco is a city of hills—some forty-two. Perhaps its most famous is Telegraph Hill, an outcropping on the northeastern shore of the San Francisco side of the Bay. Early Spanish inhabitants called this promontory Loma Alta (High Hill) when San Francisco was still a village named Yerba Buena in the 1830s. Nineteenth-century paintings and engravings show the eastern slope of Telegraph Hill already chipped away by the blasting for quarried rock to be used as ship ballast for otherwise empty vessels returning to eastern ports after bringing passengers and supplies to California, and for street paving stones for this isolated western outpost.

In 1849, two years after San Francisco took its name from the patron St. Francis of Assisi, George Sweeny and Theodore Baugh, founders of the Merchants' Exchange, built a small, 18- by 25-foot two-story house as an observation and semaphore signalling station on the summit of the hill—thereafter called Telegraph

17

Hill—to service the growing shipping industry. On top of this building they erected a "high black pole and attached to it, in such a manner as to be raised or lowered at pleasure, ... two black arms."[1]

By position of these arms, this semaphore system signalled both the approach of a boat from the ocean and the type of vessel it was. For example, the signal for a side-wheel steamer (both arms extended at right angles in crucifix position) brought crowds rushing to the wharf to greet friends and hear the latest news from the East or to the post office for the mail.

A ludicrous incident, illustrating the familiarity of everybody with the signal, occurred at one of the theaters [the American Theater] . . . The play was Sheridan's *Hunchback* and the house was crowded from pit to dome. Julia had quarreled with Clifford, when Master Walter, dressed in black which showed in bold relief against the light walls of the drawing-room, excitedly rushed on the stage and throwing out his arms exclaimed, "What does this mean?" For a moment there was no response, when a voice from the gallery roared out, "Side-wheel steamer!" The effect was electrical. The house burst into shouts of laughter; and for many minutes Master Walter could not get on with his speech.[2]

Later this inner signal station on Telegraph Hill became part of a more elaborate system involving an outer signal station off the Pacific coast at Point Lobos, linking Point Reyes to the north, Point San Pedro to the south, and the Farallon Islands to the west.

By 1853 an electric telegraph system had supplanted the semaphore. But because the signal had been of such value to the young city, some shippers, merchants, and other public-minded citizens, wishing to insure the preservation of the telegraph station as a landmark, purchased the property on the summit of Telegraph Hill, named it Pioneer Park, and donated it to the City of San Francisco in 1876, to be kept an open space.

Colorful Lillie Coit

Parallel with the establishing of Telegraph Hill was the dashing life of Lillie Hitchcock Coit, who came to San Francisco in 1851 at the age of seven from Maryland with her Army surgeon father and her Southern plantation-

Lillie Hitchcock with her father

belle mother. Not long after her arrival, young Lillie Hitchcock was involved in one of San Francisco's early disastrous fires when she and several playmates were in a vacant house which began to burn. Though she managed to escape, two others were not so fortunate.

In the 1850s firemen were a special breed in San Francisco. They were "the best men" in the city, grouping in volunteer companies usually made up of lawyers, doctors, bankers, and merchants. There were the usual benevolent societies of the nineteenth century in San Francisco as well, but nothing seemed as glamorous as the red-shirted firemen with shining black peaked caps and black trousers stuffed into high black boots. These handsome young men with their polished hand-drawn fire engines had a difficult time struggling up the un-paved city hills to put out fires in this city which endured six major conflagrations before the famous earthquake and fire of 1906.

Legend says that one afternoon on her way home from school, teen-aged Lillie Hitchcock came upon short-staffed Knickerbocker Engine Company No. 5 of the Volunteer Fire Department pulling its engines up Telegraph Hill to reach a fire. Remembering her childhood experience, Lillie threw down her schoolbooks and rallied some male bystanders to help as she herself began hauling on the tow rope shouting, "Come on, you men, pull!" No. 5 raced up the hill and was the first engine to douse the fire. After that, Lillie became the mascot of No. 5, wearing an honorary uniform, smoking cigars, and playing poker with the men all night. She proudly sported a gold diamond-studded fireman's badge reading "No. 5," awarded her in 1863. For the rest of her life, she signed her initials LHC5, and, even in death, at her cremation at age 86, Lillie wore the famous badge.

In 1863 Lillie Hitchcock married Howard Coit, a wealthy caller at the old San Francisco Stock and Exchange Board, of whom Helen Holdredge writes in *Firebelle Lillie*, "tall, distinguished Howard Coit in his impeccable attire, the intimate friend of the giants of industry and empire building."[3] However, her parents were not very pleased with this marriage of their only child to Coit, scion of an old Connecticut family. After Coit died in 1885 at age 47 of heart trouble, Lillie Coit spent most of her life in France, becoming a favorite of the court of Napoleon III. Curiously, before she left for Europe she expressed a desire to buy the property on top of Telegraph Hill, her old neighborhood, as a gift to San Francisco; she must have been surprised to learn that the city already owned Pioneer Park.

Lillie Hitchcock as a teenager

She returned briefly after the turn of the century. But in 1904 an incident in which an insane distant relative killed a man in her apartment at the old Palace Hotel and then threatened her life caused Lillie Coit once again to leave San Francisco. This time she remained in Paris for twenty years. At last coming home to her "soul city" towards the end of her life, she died in the Dante Sanatorium in 1929. Childless, Lillie Hitchcock Coit left two-thirds of her fortune to the Universities of California and Maryland. And as tangible evidence of her affection for San Francisco, she bequeathed the remaining third to the City and County of San Francisco "to be expended in an appropriate manner for the purpose of adding to the beauty of the city which I have always loved."

The Politics of Funding

Lillie Coit's heartfelt bequest became the golden apple of discord for those who were to execute the directions of the will during the following four years. In January 1931, when the Board of Supervisors first proposed the expenditure of the money on the construction of a roadway around Lake Merced, two of the three executors of Lillie Coit's estate protested, since she had never mentioned a personal memorial either in life or in her will but had left the funds for general civic beautification. They requested instead that the Board find "ways and means of expending this money on a memorial that in itself would be an entity and not a unit of public development."[4]

Herbert Fleishhacker, both a member of the Board of Supervisors and President of the Board of Park Commissioners, was among those present at the Supervisors' meeting at which the members "informally and not by resolution, unanimously consented to the creation of a Coit Advisory Committee, to advise as to the disposition of the Coit bequest." He thereupon wrote to the Board of Supervisors requesting that they "make funds available

Lillie Hitchcock Coit as
an honorary member
of Knickerbocker
Engine Co. No. 5

from the Coit Bequest for the construction of a memorial for the beautification of Telegraph Hill." In view of Lillie Coit's earlier attempt to buy Pioneer Park for San Francisco, this choice seemed very appropriate.

The executors then approved the "beautification" under the supervision of the Park Commissioner (i.e., Fleishhacker himself). Thus by April 1931, Fleishhacker as President of the Commission, and John McLaren, Director of Golden Gate Park, were to act for the Park Commission on the specifically formed Coit Advisory Committee. By September, city funds expanded to $125,000 the original $118,000 specified by the Coit will; the Committee had approved and authorized a model of a monument depicting the original volunteer fire department by sculptor Haig Patigian for the parking lot; they had also unanimously authorized him to "prepare a suitable plaque for installation on the Memorial Tower on Telegraph Hill . . . not to exceed the sum of $1,000" subject to their approval; and they had requested Commissioner James B. McSheehy to "cause the rezoning of the property in the vicinity of Telegraph Hill so that skyscrapers in the future would not interfere with the view from or detract from the beauty of the Coit Memorial."

The Construction of Coit Tower

Various artists submitted schemes in a competition for the final form of the memorial itself. Among them were a "long, horizontal mass"—Patigian's plan for a huge sculpture; a monumental column with a figure on top by Renato Corte; and the winner, the proposal of a single elevated tower drawn by Henry Howard in the office of prominent architect Arthur Brown, Jr. (who had designed the neo-classical City Hall and War Memorial Opera House in Civic Center).

Henry Howard, son of famed architect John Galen Howard and brother to three artists and an architect sister, undertook the major design tasks of Coit Tower. He had to meet the esthetic problems posed by an asymmetrically formed hill as the base of the tower, its scale, and the various viewpoints caused by that geographic asymmetry. Furthermore, he had to stay within the budget of $125,000—not a great amount, even in 1932. The cheapest building material turned out to be reinforced concrete; even the wooden forms were resold later to another builder at a profit for the city.

The selection of the memorial tower was not a unanimous act of the newly formed Art Commission whose job it was to pass the final judgment. As late as 1946, Gertrude Atherton, herself a talented author, a spirited San Franciscan, and a good friend of Lillie Coit, wrote with some bitterness in *My San Francisco: A Wayward Biography* that Lillie Coit had intended that the money be expended in her name in a manner which would add to the beauty of San Francisco.

Postcard aerial view of Coit Tower and approach

But alas!

I was a member of the Art Commission when the different models and drawings were submitted to it for approval. None was adequate in my opinion nor in that of Mrs. Musante—the only other woman on the Commission—but the model of the tower by the eminent architect Arthur Brown met with the final approval of the men. Mrs. Musante and I protested in vain; men always stand by other men against women, and after days of wrangling the males of the Commission went into a huddle and emerged with the dictum that they were for the Coit Tower, and that was that. They were very polite about it, and there was nothing for two lone females to do but sulk. So there it stands, insulting the landscape. Lily [sic] Hitchcock deserved a better memorial.[5]

The crowning irony seemed to be that although the site itself was quite appropriate, Lillie Hitchcock Coit, said Atherton, had an aversion to towers!

As the Tower began to take shape, some outraged local artists appealed to the Art Commission to halt the construction, arguing on esthetic grounds that the finished monument would be two-thirds as tall as the hill itself. (The elevation of Telegraph Hill is 288 feet; as it stands today, the Tower rises 180 feet above a rectangular base 32 feet high, despite Commissioner Lewis Byington's "fixed opinion," which he read into the Park Commission minutes,[6] that Coit Tower should be at least 250 feet high.) The artists also claimed that the building was a mockery because they assumed (as do many today) that architects Brown and Howard had designed the monument in the shape of a fire hose nozzle in memory of Lillie Coit's fondness for the Fire Department, an intention that the architects consistently denied.

However, there was no stopping the construction, despite the opinions of Gertrude Atherton, Mrs. Musante, the dissenting artists, and the 464 people who signed the artists' petition against building Coit Tower. Time was of the essence, for according to the Park Commission minutes,

Mr. Fleishhacker stressed the point that in order to prevent further delay in construction and a possible future controversy with the Art Commission about to be created, it would be well to sign a contract and have the work actually started prior to January 8. 1932, The other members of the Committee were also of the same opinion.[7]

Fleishhacker worked with the speed and efficiency of one who is used to doing things both expeditiously and profitably. He had risen to a high position in the business world through shrewd buying and selling of commodities useful to the expanded California frontier. Beginning as a salesman for his father's paper manufacturing company after completing grade school and one year of commercial courses, by 1907 he had had business triumphs in flour, lumber, electric power, and, most outstandingly, banking. Interested in art and civic affairs, he accepted an appointment to the Park Commission offered by Mayor James Rolph, Jr., where his "Midas touch" helped him to breeze through public life as he had through business. His interest in the public sector culminated in such projects as the Fleishhacker Zoo and the Mother House on its grounds. He also helped to secure funds for the War Memorial Opera House, the Veterans' Building, and Aquatic Park.[8]

After the building company Young and Horstmeyer was successful in submitting the lowest bid for the construction of Coit Tower (theirs was $77,398 versus the highest bid of $95,000 by Anderson and Ringrose, among the fifteen offered), it was natural that the Portland Cement Association, in which Fleishhacker had a considerable financial interest, would supply the 5,000 barrels of cement and the 3,200 cubic yards of concrete needed for the fabrication of the monument.

Despite Fleishhacker's desire for the continuing speed of construction, various delays caused the work to stretch out during most of 1933, even with a crew numbering between fifty and seventy-five workers. The engineering aspects of Brown and Howard's model did not pose any problems. Brown was very experienced, having planned many public buildings in San Francisco, particularly in Civic Center. He was a successful architect, a good designer, a quiet but competent man who, with his partner, John Bakewell, Jr., had been a top student at the Ecole de Beaux Arts in Paris before the turn of the century. Harold Gilliam wrote in *The San Francisco Experience* that according to his teacher, renowned architect Bernard Maybeck, Brown had "perfect taste."[9]

Although Brown never published his inspiration for a tower design rather than a horizontal mass or a large sculpture, some have likened it to the towers of medieval fortresses built in Europe on hills similar to Telegraph Hill, others to Persian towers, and still others to a huge "replica of the Column of Progress at the Panama-Pacific Exposition of 1915."[10] In an article in *Architect and Engineer*, Henry Howard explained their thinking: he stated that the Tower was a bold but "simple fluted shaft" with a roughish, uniform texture to be built of reinforced concrete throughout.

In that 1933 article, Howard said of the lack of precedent:

The tower has no prototype. It is not a medieval keep to resist capture, nor a lighthouse to warn off mariners. Neither is it a clock tower nor a fanciful ebullition for an exposition. It is intended to be dignified with austerity; monumental without utilitarian function.[11]

About the exterior fluted design:

It was found the shallow flutes gave a sturdier effect and one which contrasted better with the system of arches at the top. The effect attained by the play of light and shades in these arches combined with the glimpses of the sky through the openings in the top ring is perhaps the most original element of the whole composition. By night it offers great possibilities for artificial lighting effects.[12]

Although Howard spoke of Coit Tower's having had no design precedent, architects of the day were quite interested in a twentieth-century phenomenon flourishing in Europe: the esthetically designed power station. Fuel and power stations had been regarded as unavoidable nui-

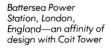

Battersea Power Station, London, England—an affinity of design with Coit Tower

Coit Tower's only adornment at its dedication—the phoenix bird symbolizing San Francisco's repeated growth after its many fires

sances in the urban scene. However, because these power plants were so large and conspicuous, prominent architects in such countries as Germany, Hungary, Holland, and England took on the job of creating unobtrusive but pleasing energy-generating leviathans. Sir Giles Gilbert Scott was in the process of doing just that in the early 1930s for London's south bank: the Battersea Power Station. His building took the shape of a veritable cathedral of brick, with "a sequence of articulated rectangular forms"[13] as bases for four tall fluted chimneys which were "as pleasant to look at as many campaniles."[14] Thus Howard had at least a spiritual paradigm, if not a "direct prototype," in London.

The architects' original interior plans had called for a restaurant in the Tower. However, they later substituted for it a public space to be used for displaying pictures, paintings, and exhibits of San Francisco's pioneer days, in keeping with the history of Pioneer Park. To the left of the entrance is a plaque by Haig Patigian commemorating Lillie Coit's bequest. Above two miniature fluted columns flanking the exterior entrance, sculptor Robert B. Howard cast a high relief plaque four feet in diameter of the phoenix bird with wings outspread.[15] Bundled fasces on either side commemorate Lillie Coit's connection with the Fire Department. This adornment, which Brown commissioned during construction of the unpainted grey monument, was its only decoration when the Coit Memorial Tower was dedicated to the City of San Francisco on October 8, 1933.

Dedication program cover

NEW DEAL SUPPORT
OF THE ARTS

The Public Works of Art Project, 1933–34

LILLIE Coit's death in July 1929 had occurred just three months before the disastrous economic crash that shocked and crippled the nation. Four years later, the economy had still not rallied to the level of prosperity of pre-crash days. The art world was also in crisis. The prices and sales of the prosperous 1920s fell to a depressingly low level. In his book *The New Deal for Artists*, Richard D. McKinzie descibes the ailing national scene: "A 165 market price index for art in 1929 had shriveled to 50 by 1933. Art importation was down over 80 percent and the production of artists' materials was off by almost half."[1] The image of the starving artist was now more than just a romantic notion.

In both the ancient world and Europe, government support of artists had a long and productive history, dating back to the sponsorship of murals by Egyptian pharoahs for their greater glory in the next world. Monarchies and the Church had commissioned artists and sculptors to adorn buildings in the Middle Ages and in the Renaissance. While government patronage of the arts was not new, it had never existed in the United States as an economic fact of life.

Thus in 1933 an artist with impeccable credentials proposed a novel idea to heal the financial malaise to which the American art world had succumbed. He was George Biddle, a classmate of President Franklin D. Roosevelt and a member of a socially prominent Philadelphia family, who had given up a law career to pursue art. He had been impressed by the 1920s art movement in Mexico: President Alvaro Obregon had put to work a number of young artists to decorate public buildings in Mexico City, illustrating aspects of the Mexican revolution. For this work the painters had received low but dependable government-funded wages as civil servants. Biddle noted particularly the fusion of art and political philosophy as demonstrated in the works of the "Big Three" Mexican mural artists: Jose Clemente Orozco, David Alfaro Siqueiros, and Diego Rivera.

Biddle wrote to his old fellow schoolmate from Groton and Harvard, President Roosevelt, asking that American artists be employed to paint murals depicting the social ideals of the new administration and contemporary life on the walls of public buildings.

Roosevelt, newly elected, was just launching the nationwide New Deal. He put Biddle in touch with Assistant Secretary of the Treasury Lawrence Robert, the "custodian of federal buildings." Robert informed Biddle that a department in charge of decorating federal buildings had existed since 1910, but in fact this adornment had usually been of the Federal Classic style which was so traditionally architectural that it was hardly distinguishable from the structures it embellished. Secretary Robert was sympathetic to Biddle's innovative ideas for contemporary art in government buildings in Washington, D.C.—but they both had to do battle with the conservative National Commission of Fine Arts, which favored the neo-classical pattern of the past. At this point Robert sought counsel of a colleague in the Treasury Department, Edward Bruce, who was recommended by Florence Kahn, a Congresswomen from California.

It is probably safe to say that Edward Bruce, at once a lawyer, a silver expert, a stockbroker, a businessman,

Members of the Tower art executive committee; detail from Library

and, most importantly, a professional painter himself, became so enthusiastic about supporting American art in the public domain that he might be called "Mr. New Deal Art." Applying the Mexican mural concept to American government buildings was appealing enough for Bruce to establish a new funding agency, under the auspices of the Treasury Department, to disburse the traditional 1% of building costs allotted for art. With money from the recently created Civil Works Administration, he established the Public Works of Art Project (PWAP), which anticipated financing some 2,500 artists and 500 laborers in an American artistic renaissance.

Bruce had three things in mind: first, to support professional artists and thereby create quality art; second, to educate the public to appreciate the art thus generated; and third, to please the patron (i.e., the U.S. Government) without threatening patriotism or violating conventional art traditions (i.e., produce nothing too avant-garde or left-leaning). A sympathetic yet shrewd prime mover, Bruce knew that he had to win the support of both the "establishment" art circles and the general public. Toward this end, he appointed sixteen regional chairmen who were usually directors of established museums in their communities. The chairmen's major job would be to promote an egalitarian art style and subject matter the average citizen could understand and accept.

Another brilliant move on Bruce's part was to select an active and respected art critic and editor as technical director for PWAP—Forbes Watson. He was to become so dedicated to the cause of New Deal art that he wrote copiously and eloquently on the philosophy of government-supported art, social history, and public esthetics. Bruce and Watson wrote hundreds of pages of communiques, personal letters, bulletins, reports, and even books reinforcing their common theme. Always they had in mind, as Bruce stated in an open letter to artists early in 1934, that the artist should "sell to the American people the idea that art is and should be an integral part of our civilization."

The market-place imagery in Bruce's statement was not accidental. He was mindful of "cost accountability," a very American concept to which he was philosophically committed. Unlike the Works Project Administration

(WPA) with its subdivision called the Federal Art Project (FAP), which came into being about a year later and was sometimes characterized as "a relief project for starving artists,"[2] the PWAP was a pilot program which solicited the work of artists through selection by regional committees. The artists received wages ranging from $25 to $45 per week to work about thirty hours, as one official wrote to them, "in your studio and without dictation from anyone."[3]

The speed with which both policy and operation developed amazes those who today are familiar with bureaucratic lags and delays. Here is Forbes Watson paying homage in 1938 to Edward Bruce, whom he called "the fountain-head of all that the United States had done for art in the past five years [since 1933]":

When the whole thing started I worked with him day and night. It was December 8, 1933. A meeting was called. Mrs. Roosevelt [et al.] were there . . . a dozen museum directors from all parts of the country, Ned Bruce, and myself. On the 12th of December, four days later, an office was in full swing in the Treasury Department, the first artists were on the payroll, sixteen regional chairmen, directing regions which included the entire country, had been appointed, and a system, new to the world, had been evolved for employing artists. This dynamic change was a one-man affair.[4]

As for prime mover George Biddle, he went on to paint his murals called *Life Ordered with Justice* in the Justice Department building in Washington, D.C., under the later Section of Fine Arts.[5] Artists of the New Deal owed him a great debt of gratitude.

The PWAP in San Francisco

San Francisco became District 15 of the national plan. On December 10, 1933, Edward Bruce telegraphed Dr. Walter Heil, newly arrived from Germany and the director of the de Young Museum in Golden Gate Park: "A central committee [for District 15] will be set up in San Francisco and we hope that you will accept the position [of chair] of this committee to supervise the work done in Northern California and Nevada."[6] It would be Heil's task to select and supervise "worthy artists" and to choose appropriate public buildings to embellish.

Edward Bruce, Eleanor Roosevelt, Assistant Secretary of the Treasury L.W. Robert, and Forbes Watson, Technical Director of the PWAP

Buildings! Suddenly there was a new use for Coit Memorial Tower, now two months old. Instead of pioneer memorabilia, it would house murals executed by master artists under PWAP. An executive committee, chaired by Dr. Heil, and composed of Thomas Carr Howe, Jr. (assistant director, California Palace of the Legion of Honor Museum), Charles Stafford Duncan (a commercial artist), and Col. Harold Mack (a stockbroker), was formed. They were assisted by a blue-ribbon advisory group of prominent citizens and artists, whose members were Templeton Crocker, Mrs. Lewis P. Hobart (wife of the architect of Grace Cathedral and the Bohemian Club), Capt. B.F. Lamb, Mrs. Oscar Sutro, Edgar Walter (a prominent sculptor), and architect Arthur Brown, Jr.

At the second committee meeting Dr. Heil asked Tower architect Arthur Brown, Jr., whether he was "generally in favor" of decorating the inside of Coit Tower with murals. "I think so, yes," replied Brown. "The primitive nature of the Coit Tower would lend itself to that sort of thing better than other public buildings."[7] At this meeting, a major theme, a set palette of colors, and a consistent scale of proportion were approved. Dr. Heil was anxious to begin as soon as possible since guaranteed funding under PWAP existed for only two months, later extended to June 1934.

Meeting in the Anglo California National Bank, the committee and its advisors reached a consensus about the impending art project: the committee surely could whitewash out whatever they didn't like politically or felt was inartistically executed in this untried pilot project of mural art at Coit Tower! As it turned out, however, that policy was very difficult to execute when controversy did develop upon completion of the project some six months later.

At the same time that Bruce and Heil were making national and local policy, the artists of San Francisco, in desperation over their economic plight during the Depression, undertook what they thought was independent action—although it turned out to be exactly parallel to that of the PWAP. Bernard B. Zakheim, one of the artists selected to paint in Coit Tower, remembered it this way years later:

I was in Paris in 1932 having an "artist's sabbatical" when I read about the plight of the artists in the United States unable to find employment in their media. I invited my fellow American artists, the "Guggenheim Stars" I called them, as they were on fellowships, to my studio at 111 rue de Orleans to lay plans for funding a federal art project at home. When I returned to San Francisco I won a competition to do the fresco at the Jewish Community Center; I had recently done one in Hungary. Because of my prestige with the Center mural, I was able to call a meeting of my fellow artists, supported by my friend, poet Kenneth Rexroth. The first meeting was at the Whitcomb Hotel on Market Street. I was chairing the meeting and I told the artists about local sculptor Beniamino Bufano threatening to commit suicide, and local artist Sergei Sherbakoff, who had an exhibit of his paintings at the Legion of Honor while he was on a CWA project cleaning the toilets below the exhibit hall.

We decided to call a bigger meeting at local artist Maynard Dixon's studio; sculptor Ralph Stackpole was there, and he knew someone in Washington—Edward Bruce, an artist-banker. We made a collection of small change—less than a dollar—and sent a night letter to Washington. The result was that Dr. Walter Heil, Thomas Carr Howe, Charles Stafford Duncan, and Col. Harold Mack were appointed locally to form a committee to create an art project, with Dr. Heil as chairman. My idea was to decorate the bandstand shell in the Mall in Golden Gate Park and other outdoor places, but at that time Herbert Fleishhacker was under sharp criticism about his "last erection," the Coit Tower. So he corralled the project to put art work into the Tower in order to justify its existence.[8]

Unaware of Bruce's efforts already in progress, the artists were truly amazed to receive a strongly positive reply from Washington in only four days!

Architect Arthur Brown, Jr., holding plans of Coit Tower in front of City Hall, from a mural at the Beach Chalet, San Francisco, by Lucien Labaudt

THE STORY OF
THE MURALS

The Triumph of Fresco as a Medium

WHAT had begun as a tentative suggestion by Dr. Heil to Arthur Brown, Jr., about murals at Coit Tower gradually emerged as a star project in Heil's mind. In a letter to Edward Rowan, the Assistant Technical Director of the PWAP in Washington, D.C., Heil championed the Coit Tower as "our *pièce de resistance.*" He described centralizing "the efforts of some of our best painters on one main project" atop Telegraph Hill, "a vantage point constantly visited by local residents and tourists."

The interior of this building, with its simple architectural planes and line, offers a particularly fortunate field for decoration in *fresco*. It is this medium which, during the last years, has become increasingly popular with the younger artists in San Francisco, so that a considerable number of them are available for this work. We are reasonably sure that their work will be both creditable as art and characteristic of what we may call the "San Francisco School of Painting." The interior, being broken up into various individual walls, allows us to assign comparatively small areas to individual artists who

33

can both design and execute their mural within a limited time. The artists themselves are enthused about this project and show a most encouraging spirit of cooperation. . . . Altogether twenty-six artists are so far at work on this project.[1]

It was Heil who proposed the ancient medium of fresco (earth colors applied to wet plaster directly on the wall) for Coit Tower. Perhaps he was influenced by the enthusiasm of some of the artists who had recently worked in Mexico with Diego Rivera and wanted now to employ his style and approach to subject matter. Heil, seeing the idea in historic terms and possibly thinking of the longevity of Egyptian and classical frescoes still extant, said: "There is no reason why Coit Memorial Tower with its mural paintings should not stand five hundred to one thousand years from now, a monument to this epoch and to the artists who worked on it."

Much of the enthusiasm and *esprit de corps* among the artists at Coit Tower seemed to be generated by the medium of fresco. As Dr. Heil put it, "The technique of fresco is, in itself, a unifying influence. . . . The artists

Slaking the plaster to prepare it for application to a wall

Diego Rivera and assistant Emmy Lou Packard applying earth pigments to wet plaster in previously sketched area on Pan-American Unity by Diego Rivera, created at Golden Gate International Exposition, 1940; now on view at City College of San Francisco

established for themselves one scale and also one palette consisting of elementary earth colors."

The fresco painters at the Tower followed the old Italian tradition as the Mexican artists interpreted it. In this process, fine marble dust is mixed with slaked (pronounced "slacked") lime to create the painting surface. Plasterers slake the lime by firing it quickly in kilns, then soaking it in water—historically, in pits in the ground, but nowadays in large vats—for about three months.

In *fresco buono*, the plasterer prepares the wall by building up a bed of cement and rough lime plaster on which the artist traces an outline or cartoon of the design. Early on the morning of the day that the artist is to paint, the plasterer spreads a thin smooth surface coat of fine wet plaster about two feet square, approximately in the shape of the outlined figures. Using a very small wet brush, the artist applies the earth colors, either dry or mixed with distilled water, repeatedly building up their intensity as long as the surface remains moist—up to twelve hours. Although it appears a solid color to the eye, under a microscope the fresco surface shows eight particles of white plaster "cupping" one color particle. To assure their uniformity, only one artist-assistant at Coit

*Spraying water on
the wet plaster to
ensure its moistness*

Tower, Farwell Taylor, ground all the color pigments for all
the frescoes.

In *fresco secco*, the medium Jane Berlandina used
in the egg tempera room on the second floor, the final
plaster surface is allowed to dry. The artist may then use
any of several media besides water: casein, oil paint,
gums and resins, as well as egg tempera. Some artists
begin a *buono* and then intensify by superimposing a
secco colors.

Thus, as the color dries in or on the plaster, the
picture becomes part of the wall; any changes must be
chipped out, for there is no altering or rubbing out once
the design is begun. Although painted quickly in small
sections, fresco lends itself to bold, direct designs, usually
of free, simplified, and often vigorous forms and vivid
colors, albeit limited by the earth color palette. Zakheim,
for one, finding it a very exciting medium in which to
work, likened the application of the brush on wet plaster
to the bestowal of a kiss—not surprising when one re-

members that the very word fresco is from the Italian *a fresco:* "fresh."

The physical labor involved in fresco painting is more taxing than one might suppose. Zakheim described it as follows:

Each artist had assistants who had other assistants for manual work. The master artists did the design; the assistant, also an artist, helped by delivering materials pertaining to this section, because the thing had to be pretty intensely made. A fresco has to be finished in a certain time; otherwise it has to be chopped out. So an artist's assistant is very important because he has to know from the artist which colors have to be prepared [by grinding the earth pigments on a marble slab] for that given section which is going to be done in that given time and help out right along. Only a trained artist could really be an assistant —and these were. But the master artist remains the artist who does the actual work. The assistants must be well aware of what you need, how you are working, keep the palette for you all the time or change the color on the palette, because there's a time factor as the wet plaster dries. I worked on the wet plaster directly, although everybody else painted on a black wash or a cross-hatched network of black lines first, and then upon the black put the other colors, thus guaranteeing uni-

Lucien Labaudt at work on Powell Street; note "Wed" where he is painting on that day

formity. When the mural is finished, the black guarantees that nothing will come out too strong. But I like a more spontaneous approach.[2]

Although the creation of fresco is spontaneous, its restoration is tedious. In theory, since the pigments are of the earth, there should be no organic disintegration. However, water or moisture may accumulate behind the fresco surface, causing deterioration; if outdoors, wind can erode it; scratches, even small ones, can remove the paint, causing the white plaster to show; "preservatives" such as shellac or varnish are sometimes mistakenly applied, thus preventing the normal "breathing" of frescoes; and retouching with such incompatible materials as oil paint will contaminate the fragile surface and can cause further peeling. If the fresco is left alone, the marbleizing process eventually forms a surface "crystal."

Bernard Zakheim
with assistant Julia
H. Rogers

Thus, sometimes it is better not to restore at all rather than do it incorrectly.

Other Media

Exciting as the fresco technique was for most of the artists at Coit Tower, not all shared this passion, which was particularly demanding and required an *in situ* communal effort that the more traditional or academic artists disliked. When Dr. Heil first approached Otis Oldfield, a respected artist and teacher at the San Francisco School of Fine Arts, to participate in the project, Oldfield refused, saying that he would rather work alone in his own studio. Heil then suggested that Oldfield create an oil painting on canvas for the small lobby in front of the elevator leading to the top of the Tower, and that he supervise the work of three other artists of his own choosing as well. Oldfield agreed, providing that they could each work in their own studios using oil on canvas, the completed paintings to be installed in the arch-topped lunettes in the lobby. Heil accepted this arrangement, and Oldfield invited his friends Jose Moya del Pino, Rinaldo Cuneo, and William Gaw to paint scenes of San Francisco Bay, using a different color palette from that of the frescoes in the outer corridors, and a smaller scale. When William Gaw had to withdraw during the initial planning stages because of an economic conflict, Rinaldo Cuneo painted Gaw's panel as well as his own, for, as Mrs. Oldfield remembered, "he was a fast painter, faster than the others."[3] As a result, there are four large and three small oil lunettes in the lobby, complementary to one another, as are the fresco panels on the other walls.

Jane Berlandina's use of egg tempera contrasts with the syle of the other Coit Tower murals

The art in one final room is quite different from both fresco and oil—in medium, subject matter, and style. It is the little room on the second floor that Jane Berlandina, wife of the Tower architect Henry Howard, chose to decorate in neither a formal academic style nor that of Rivera. She used a silhouette approach in egg tempera (egg-yolk based paint applied to dry plastered walls) with a limited palette of shades of chartreuse, russet, and brown, with white outlines reminiscent of the "calligraphic" technique of her teacher and fellow French artist, Raoul Dufy. The four walls make up a little "house," portraying scenes from home life.

The Themes of the Frescoes

By January 5, 1934, Heil had already screened the sketches of about fifty applicants, reducing the final choices to the twenty-six he felt best qualified. Next he asked Victor Arnautoff, whose name had come up in the December meeting with Brown, to serve as group director or foreman, "to coordinate the scale and palette in cooperation with this committee." In addition, Arnautoff was to keep an eye on the subject matter of the frescoes, which was to be "the contemporary American scene in all its various aspects." Brown had suggested specifically San Francisco scenes; a sort of compromise resulted in aspects of California life, with the depiction of "industrial production in one wing, food production and agriculture in another, and the City life resulting from both in a third." The fifteen artists who painted these frescoes on the first floor followed Brown's recommendation that the work be composed in a unified whole, not "in patches or pieces."

To bridge the lobby oils and the five second-floor outdoor recreational life frescoes, Lucien Labaudt, a San Francisco artist and dress designer with a flair for elegance and charm, asked if he might depict both sides of fashionable Powell Street on the walls of the interior staircase. Thus, as it has turned out, the palette, the media, the scale, and, above all, the subject matter have combined to create a singularly unified effect. Coit Tower was indeed the *pièce de resistance* of District 15. It is so successful that many visitors assume that one artist painted all the frescoes, and another artist all the oils!

Artistic Harmony

What impressed many people during the painting at Coit Tower was the complete harmony which pervaded the work and the communality of these artists. Nadia Navrova, writing for the *Christian Science Monitor*,[4] said it reminded her of a guild of medieval craftsmen adorning a cathedral—almost in anonymity. After all, here were twenty-six master painters with their nineteen assistants, themselves artists, creating collectively three-quarters of the fresco painting that existed in California at that time —and under one roof.

There were few interpersonal problems; the "purists" (sometimes referred to as "ivory tower artists" by the more publicly oriented painters) created their preliminary sketches and layouts in their own studios, or in the case of the oil-lunette artists, the completed canvases. One or two others preferred to do their actual painting on location after the others had left for the day. The artists put in their thirty hours a week as they chose, often working into the small hours to meet the demands of the rapidly

Victor Arnautoff with assistant Tom Hayes (kneeling)

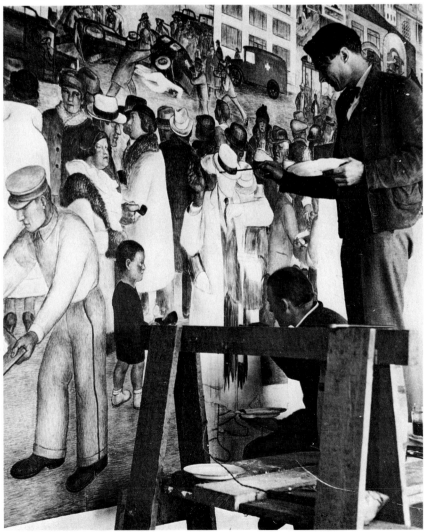

drying plaster, then taking the next day off. Surprised at
their diligence, Col. Mack went back to Washington to
report that the artists at Coit Tower were very moral and
conscientious, not drunken, promiscuous, and orgiastic
as some—including Brig. Gen. William Brady, a kindly
but officious World War I VFW caretaker at the Tower
—had predicted a group of Bohemians would be!

Costs and Technical Assistance

The artists worked very hard to earn their average wage
of $31.22 per week. The total art project, including the bill
for materials, the two full-time plasterers,[5] the laborers
who prepared the heavy materials, the artists' assistants,
and the master artists themselves, cost $24,300, produc-
ing 3,691 square feet of painted wall surface in six
months' time. (As an example, Zakheim earned $619.27
for four sketches, 94 square feet of wall space, and fif-
teen-and-a-half weeks of labor.[6])

In keeping with national PWAP policy, local government contributed a portion of the cost, both to ease the
financial burden on the federal budget and to insure a
certain amount of pride of local investment. Thus the San
Francisco Park Commission donated $900 to cover the
cost of sandblasting the walls at the Tower in preparation
for the frescoes, and provided rent-free quarters for the
office of the regional committee.

By today's standards the wages paid the artists especially seem rather low (about a dollar an hour); however,
what Edward Bruce wrote in March 1934 about the national scene applied to San Francisco as well:

There has been no criticism or carping from the artists as to the
amount being paid them by the government. . . . Instead,
there have been almost unanimous expressions of gratitude
for the employment and of the happiness that the artists feel in
the assurance of a living wage with the opportunity to work at
the things they love to do—and the added pleasure that the
work is wanted for the embellishment of public buildings.[7]

And if the standard of achievement at Coit Tower is any
criterion, the artists, the public, and the government all
benefited greatly from this particular investment of
money, time, and talent.

POLITICS, SENSATIONALISM, AND THE MURALS

WITH great enthusiasm, the artists went to work at Coit Tower at the beginning of January 1934. An editorial in the San Francisco *Chronicle* noted that the San Francisco artists displayed "tranquility in striking contrast to the skirmishes" in New York and other cities.[1] On January 16, Col. Harold Mack, representing the regional committee, wrote to Edward Rowan, a national director of PWAP, that the first and second floors of the Tower had been sandblasted and plastered and awaited the frescoes to be executed by "twenty-six master artists and ten helpers." By the end of the month, Forbes Watson, technical director in Washington, was writing to Dr. Heil stating that he was "perfectly sure the PWAP would approve of the work going forward." Both the sketches and proposed method of organization struck him as "having as fine possibilities as any project under way in any part of the country." He ended by saying that the regional committees rather than the national office would

43

be the "final arbiters" because they "know so much more about the conditions in their regions."[2]

Dr. Heil was pleased by the freedom of artistic expression, the promise of local autonomy, and, above all, the excitement of generating modern frescoes in the ancient tradition. Under the supervision of participating artist Victor Arnautoff, who also served as technical director or foreman, the work progressed according to plan. The government-appointed committee (Heil, Mack, Duncan, and Howe) rested assured that, as Col. Mack had said at the December 18 meeting, any work causing problems of any sort could be "whitewashed or discarded after it was done." There was a drive to accomplish as much as possible by February 15, the end of sure funding, though Bruce in Washington was hopeful of an extension to six months, at which time the Civil Works Administration was to end. Bruce wrote that the PWAP had existed as a "Federal project under a grant of funds from the Civil Works Administration." Local reporter John Barry wrote in his column in the San Francisco News[3] that though the PWAP in Washington had been surprised that enough fresco painters existed to "carry out plans so elaborate" as those for Coit Tower, the artists were working away in harmony. "Were there many other creative workers that could get along so well?" he asked. He credited the "dean" of the artists, Ray Boynton, who had been teaching classes in fresco painting at the School of Fine Arts (today the San Francisco Art Institute) for nearly ten years. As Heil had noted, the medium of fresco which seemed a unifying element in itself extended now to the knitting together of the designs and their execution.

The physical problems of the Tower seemed resolvable. The artists' compositions accommodated such "architectural accidents" as doorways and the "gun-slit" windows piercing the wall spaces. Lack of daylight to show Boynton's main entrance panorama could be remedied by judiciously placed artificial light. The narrow winding staircase could serve Labaudt well to show the two sides of downtown Powell Street. Some artists who had never worked in fresco before, such as sculptor Ralph Stackpole and easel painter John Langley Howard, found the new medium a challenge. Many of the artists used one another's portraits in their work since, as they said,

George Harris and Fred Olmsted, Jr., incorporating a "gun-slit" window into Banking and Law

John Langley Howard working in a medium new to him

the models were so convenient. Col. Mack, representing the regional committee, summed up the atmosphere of well-being in a compliment to the project, saying that the whole scheme was so arranged as to "produce unity." Above all, the artists sensed kindred spirits and a feeling of community among themselves.

A Disruption of Halcyon Days

But even as early as mid-February 1934 the serpent of controversy began to snake through this Garden of Eden. Its path had been laid by the destruction at the Rockefeller Center in New York of a Diego Rivera mural completed the year before. Rivera had placed a giant portrait of V.I. Lenin in that most capitalistic bastion of free enterprise. Rivera received payment for his unfinished fresco, and then his patrons suddenly destroyed the work. Among celebrities who spoke out against the destruction of the fresco, writer Lincoln Steffens said, "Capitalism could not take it." Even "establishment" painters of national renown like John Sloan spoke of it as "premeditiated art murder," although Rivera himself, back in Mexico, said he was "not surprised."[4]

The San Francisco Artists' and Writers' Union, a newly formed group with about 350 members, decided to join the nationwide protest, speaking out against this act of "outrageous vandalism and political bigotry." At a protest meeting convened in Coit Tower, muralist Maxine Albro presented a resolution, approved by the membership, regarding the destruction of the Rivera painting as "no isolated example of the prejudices of any private individual or group," but rather "an acute symptom of a growing reaction in the American culture which has threatened for years to strangle all creative effort and which is becoming increasingly menacing."[5]

Concerned now about the spread of incidents like the obliteration of the Rivera mural, the artists cited frightening examples from Europe of growing repression and censorship in Germany, France, and Austria. More than one newspaper headline chronicling all these events appear in the paintings at Coit Tower. Even the artists' February meeting has become part of the permanent record: Vidar's newspaper in his mural notes the occasion, and in Zakheim's mural Ralph Stackpole reads a newspaper whose lead proclaims, "Local Artists Protest Destruction of Rivera's Fresco."

However, the work at Coit Tower proceeded with few problems. In Suzanne Scheur's panel called *Newsgathering*, her window ledge San Francisco *Chronicle* front page announces the end of the art project in April, though some artists continued to add finishing details until June. As the project drew to a close, San Francisco's Mayor Angelo Rossi asked that the opening of the showplace be set for July 7, 1934.

The Political Climate

External events in San Francisco in 1934 were beginning to cause tremors that were to shake the artists in their Tower. All during the spring, unemployed longshoremen and their union, the International Longshoremen's Association, were in conflict with the Waterfront Employers Association at the waterfront, just a stone's throw below Coit Tower. The union grew more militant and by May decided to call a strike that "no one, not even President Roosevelt,"[6] could stop. This Pacific Maritime Strike, extending from Seattle to San Diego and supported by other unions, created a breakdown in coastal commerce, closing the port of San Francisco. By June there was tremendous pressure from business to reopen the port, and the press added its voice to all the tumult and shouting.

The *California Art Research Project* of 1937 explains that "in order to arouse public opinion against the striking workers a campaign of terror and Red baiting was resorted to."[7] As part of that campaign, the newspapers decided to make a political example of the art of Coit Tower, which as a government-funded undertaking could conceivably be called "socialistic," or in any event, pro-labor. Certain members of the press had come to view the murals and were quick to see the possibilities of fomenting a scandal for "pure sensationalism," as the artists saw it, isolating out of context several details from four frescoes on the first floor.

The Errant Artists

First, news-hungry reporters noticed that three of the four San Francisco dailies in Victor Arnautoff's scene called *City Life* were depicted on the newsstand, with the glaring omission of the San Francisco *Chronicle*, although a space was obviously allotted for it. The Artists' and Writers' Union retorted, with some amusement, that Arnautoff attributed his omission to the prominence of the *Chronicle* in Zakheim's (and presumably Scheuer's) work —hence he had felt no need for further repetition.[8] Even more galling to the local press was Arnautoff's inclusion, on another rack, of two far-left publications, *The New Masses* and *The Daily Worker*.

Next, John Langley Howard in *California Industrial Life* also represented the left-wing press by painting a miner reading the *Western Worker*, a large group of militant unemployed workers with a black man in the foreground, and "the angry faces of some gold panners glaring at some tourists" who were standing near their limousine, chauffeur and lap dog juxtaposed with a broken-down Model-T Ford and a gaunt mongrel.

In his *Library,* Bernard Zakheim seemed to invite rebuke with more radical newspapers and especially a reader (ironically, he depicted fellow artist John Langley Howard) reaching for *Das Kapital* by Karl Marx; on other shelves were books written by such proletarian authors as Erskine Caldwell, Grace Lumpkin, and Maxim Gorky.

However, it was the work of Clifford Wight, a former assistant to Diego Rivera, that received the greatest censure. Wight had painted two tall figures—a surveyor and a steelworker—on either side of a large window. Although the controversial part of his fresco is gone today, Junius Cravens, a contemporary critic, described what *used* to be there. Commenting on Wight's symbolizing some of the social and political problems of the time, Cravens said:

> Over the central window [Wight] stretched a bridge, at the center of which is a circle containing the Blue Eagle of the NRA. Over the right-hand window he stretched a segment of chain; in the circle in this case appears the legend, "In God We Trust"—symbolizing the American dollar, or I presume, Capitalism. Over the left-hand window he placed a section of woven cable and a circle framing a hammer, a sickle, and the legend "United Workers of the World" [sic; i.e., "Workers of the World, Unite"], in short, Communism.[9]

Militant workers from California Industrial Life

In addition to Cravens's information, McKinzie adds, in 1973, the following details: Wight had labeled the three panels "Rugged Individualism," "The New Deal," and "Communism," apparently as various economic alternatives for the 1930s.[10] Unlike all the other designs, which Dr. Heil had approved long before execution, Wight's had gone to Arnautoff directly on the job, where Arnautoff, in his capacity as project director, had approved them.

On June 2, the same day that the San Francisco Chamber of Commerce wrote a letter to the Industrial Association asking for help to open the strike-bound port,[11] Dr. Heil had to telegraph Forbes Watson in Washington requesting guidance in what was about to become a serious controversy. He said that some artists had "at the last minute incorporated in their murals details such as newspaper headlines and certain symbols which might be interpreted as communistic propaganda."[12] In defense of the project, he noted that the offensive elements had not been visible in the original design submission. However, although the Tower wasn't yet open to the public, "through reporters, knowledge of these things has come to the editors of influential newspapers who have warned us that they would take [a] hostile attitude towards [the] whole project unless these details be removed." Heil asked what would happen if the artists themselves refused to make changes.

Watson answered that the murals had to be completed "according to the approved design without additions," to which Edward Bruce added that "the objectionable features [must] be removed," stating that if the offending artist refused to make alterations, others in the group should do so. Finally, he said, "propaganda of this kind is hurtful to the best interests of American art and likely to discourage further government patronage."

Complicating matters, the San Francisco Art Commission during its own preview tour of the art came to the conclusion that what it saw was "in opposition to the generally accepted tradition of native Americanism."[13] Thereupon the Park Commission, caretaker of Pioneer Park, locked up Coit Tower, with the Art Commission dismissing the whole fracas as "typical Rivera publicity stunt." Presumably the members were thinking of the activities at Rockefeller Center.

In reaction to this new and unexpected action by city government, a group of local artists formed a vigilante committee, intending to storm the Tower and chisel the offensive portions out of the plaster. As a counter-move, the Artists' and Writers' Union threw a picket line around the Tower in order to support Wight and to prevent obliteration of the murals by either the vigilante group or the government.

In an article titled "A Frescoed Tower Clangs Shut Amid Gasps,"[14] Evelyn Seely described the chaotic scene: police had cut off the approach to the Tower halfway down Telegraph Hill, saying "someone might throw rocks, or give signals" to the waterfront below during the labor crisis, now on its way to becoming the General Strike that finally occurred on July 16.

Both the picketing and the police activities kept Coit Tower in the news during the early summer of 1934. To

SOVIET SYMBOL IN TOWER

An artist's rendering of the composite photo which appeared in the July 5, 1934 S.F. Examiner

insure that the news would not grow stale, one enterprising reporter for the Hearst press managed to enter the Tower, photograph the Wight hammer-and-sickle logo, and then, making a quarter-turn to his left, photograph the library scene by Zakheim. In the tranquility of his office, this reporter superimposed the logo directly above the right-hand portion of Zakheim's library mural. The doctored photo appeared with a caption reading, "Here is the painting in the Coit Memorial Tower that has caused a bitter dispute between artists and the Art Commission"; along with it was a short article correctly describing the design as placed above a large window, although the photograph obviously showed *no* window.[15] The paper was later forced to print a retraction (which it buried in the back pages several weeks later), but the bad news had been syndicated in several hundred newspapers throughout the United States and Canada.[16]

Ironically, the altered photo and the accompanying article appeared on July 5, 1934—the day San Franciscans remember as "Bloody Thursday," the most tragic moment of the waterfront strike. On that day, two union members were shot to death. Later a funeral procession of forty thousand silent men marched to the sound of muffled drumbeats up Market Street, with an honor guard of the Veterans of World War I. By agreement with the city, the workers policed their line of march; not a policeman was visible. This event was the turning point in both stepped-up strike-breaking activity and the swing of public sentiment in favor of the workers, climaxing in the General Strike eleven days later.[17]

The Battle Extended

The Art Commission still had to decide what to do about the controversial frescoes. After much dispute, the Arnautoff, Howard, and Zakheim frescoes remained intact. However, the fate of the Wight slogans was more complicated. Wight refused to alter his painting, and no other artist seemed willing to do so. The Artists' and Writers' Union protested strongly to the PWAP on the grounds of artistic integrity. In his own defense, Clifford Wight wrote to Dr. Heil and the Art Commission that he had painted "Social Change—not industrial or agricultural or scientific development—and for this reason I made a representation of this historical fact by means of three symbols [Capitalism, The New Deal, and Communism]." The symbol of Communism "is in no way an exhortation or propaganda, but a simple statement of an existing condition." He had been surprised, he said, at the reaction of the Art Commission to the designs above the windows, for although "no sketches were asked for," he had pinned up plans for the undertaking several days before he began to paint, with no objections from fellow artists nor from the "Art Chief," Arnautoff. In answer to

Artist/assistants Shirley Staschen Triest and Julia H. Rogers reflect on the Park Commission's closing of Coit Tower

Bruce's worry that Wight's action might jeopardize future governmental funding, Wight replied that he was being censored. In answer to Art Commissioner Edgar Walter's concern that the decoration appealed to only one section of the community, Wight said that the Art Commission did not object to depicting St. Francis, "who appeals to but one section of the community. The press does not attempt to conceal the facts of social change and the existence of Communism. Why should the artist be denied the freedom allowed the journalist?" he asked.[18] Ironically, Commissioner Walter, himself a sculptor, had said quite

Detail from City Life,
V. Arnautoff

innocently, at the December 18 meeting seven months earlier when the artists' sketches were reviewed, that a drawing such as Wight's certainly "has no surprises."

Edward Bruce responded to Wight's protest: "[The artists] are welcome to all the propaganda they want, but I don't see why they should do it on our money."[19] He even took pains to seek legal counsel from a Mr. Harlan (possibly Supreme Court Justice Harlan Stone) regarding the eradication of the artwork. The answer was that "the effacing or destroying of the mural in question would not give rise to a cause of action in the artist. However, to attempt to alter it may possibly result in such legal liability."[20]

History does not record nor would anyone admit who finally removed the "decoration" in question. However, when the warring sides in the waterfront dispute had come to agreement, and when the newspapers were occupied with other issues, the Coit Memorial Tower at last opened its doors to a bemused public on

October 20, 1934. Junius Cravens's comments appearing during the summer airily dismissed the controversies: "There is something about fresco painting when it is applied to the walls of public buildings that seems to breed dissention. . . . There have always been naughty little boys who drew vilifications on schoolroom walls when their teachers were not looking. Likewise, there have always been mischievous little artists who put something over while they were not being watched. Of such substance is history made."[21]

Yet on the day that Coit Tower opened, Cravens wrote with a little more humility:

A newly completed work of art is much like a fruit which still hangs, green and undeveloped, on the tree. Predictions as to its ultimate value may be made only with considerable uncertainty. Art which has survived from yesterday is still art today, but more of yesterday's near-art has perished than has survived. Who can predict what of today's art will still be living tomorrow? . . . San Francisco should be not only proud of [the Coit Tower] artists but grateful to them as well. And this not only for what they have given the city but also because of the courageous way in which they tackled such a Gargantuan problem, fraught as it was with difficulties and discouragements, and licked it—knocked it out cold.[22]

Today's visitors to Coit Tower agree with Cravens's final vote of approval.

California of the 1930s preserved for the present

A HISTORICAL OVERVIEW

VERY rarely is a work of art an instant or even a continuing success. Few of the world's most cherished creative efforts have had the good fortune, as Kenneth Clark said in *Civilization*, of the immediate and constant appeal of Michelangelo's *Creation of Adam*, for example. Masterpieces are rare, and the fickle public can accept or revile a work at one period and not another.

Though *conceived* in harmony, the art of Coit Tower seemed to be the object of dissension from its birth to its "coming of age" in recent years. The metaphorical but disparaging language of the press has been almost as creative as the art itself. An editorial in the Stockton *California Record*, July 3, 1934, titled "Red Tints on Coit Tower," spoke of "too much Rivera influence, too little originality, and far too little horse sense," calling the artists "some brush wielders" and the murals "daubings on the Coit Memorial walls." These "pigment slingers . . . concealed a knife for the goverment that fed them" by putting their "revolutionary ideas" in the Tower.

In the San Francisco *Examiner* of July 9, only four days after the doctored fresco photograph appeared, an editor wondered why the artists who were "putting up signs of the times" weren't also incorporating Mussolini's fasces, Hitler's swastika, and Japan's rising sun. Better yet, he concluded, "If the artists were seeking excitement, they could do much better by tripping over to Russia and painting the American flag on the walls of the Kremlin. Then they would get action."[1]

Columnist Junius Cravens, writing in the San Francisco *News* on July 7, spoke of Diego Rivera as that "gargantuan Mexicano" who was "the god of American fresco painters, particularly of those who careen to larboard, so to speak. In their effort to follow his brush strokes, they not only lean over toward the extreme left, but also backward." He went on to say that three of the "twenty-five or thirty artists employed by the PWAP for the hopeless task of trying to beautify the inside of Coit Tower had seen red." The three "culprits . . . were caught at it redhanded, as it were."

In the San Francisco *News* on July 10 Arthur Caylor was writing about "those old grudge fighters, Kid Kapital and Kayo Communism" and spoke of the mural controversy as having "enough other angles to supply a cubist's coal chute."

Other Reactions

The by-now-famous July 5 doctored photograph and article also aroused some members of the public. The very day it appeared, a San Francisco lawyer seized a pen to write in great consternation to Edward Bruce: "This whole [Wight-Zakheim?] mural is an insult to every decent, patriotic citizen and should be removed at the earliest possible moment. The so-called artists who depicted ideas so subversive of good government should receive nothing for their offensive work." Bruce wrote back that he was certain that Dr. Heil "will handle the situation to everybody's satisfaction [with] the possible exception of the Communists themselves."

Edward Rowan added that he thought "an artist willfully did this piece of work to get one or two things—have his mural destroyed so that he would be in a class with Rivera, whether his aesthetic put him there or not, and to be given a lot of newspaper publicity." Rowan himself decided that the mural's "aesthetic content is practically nil. Several of the heads are well conceived but it does not excite me from the standpoint of design or composition." Presumably he was talking about the Zakheim fresco, on which the Wight slogan had been superimposed.

Even as early as May, 1934, Forbes Watson, Technical Director for the PWAP, had been on the defensive about the Mexican influence on the art at the Tower. In answer to a fairly mild comment made by by a Francis McComas of Pebble Beach, who said the painters and students were "doing a fine job" at Coit Tower on work with "a very decided Ribera [sic] influence," and supposed Rivera to be "as good as anybody," Watson responded: "I join with you in regretting the Rivera influence in our fresco painting. I think he has been infinitely overrated, and is a thoroughly bad influence for Americans."

Achieving Balance

Artist Glenn Wessels, writing in the San Francisco *Argonaut* on July 13, took a more balanced approach. He noted that a mural "should be epic in nature," symbolizing "the feelings, the beliefs, the essential spirit of a race, a nation, a society, or a group." Thus the artist is a "public servant rather than an independent individual and is limited by the belief and understanding of the multitude." He wrote also that "these murals are a little too easily understood." Praising the "unified communal spirit" of the project, he hoped the public mural artist would remain "upon the plane of high generalities with which a majority can agree, unless his purpose is dissension."

Subsequent Reactions

That the press remained moderately hostile to the art at Coit Tower is apparent in a question that the San Francisco *Chronicle* asked in 1953: "Is this art or merely grotesque rebellion of starved souls against the existing order?"[2] The artists, deeply cut, insisted their work was a mirror of American life, not a radical manifesto. As late as 1968,

Cooperation on the canning line; detail from Industries of California

one tourist guide still spoke of "the rather grim Depression-day murals executed by WPA [*sic*] artists."[3]

For one reporter the panoply at Coit Tower was incomplete. Discussing the closing of the Tower in 1934, Evelyn Seely wrote: "In the main, [the artists] presented California as powerful and productive, its machines well-oiled, its fields and orchards bountiful, its people happy in the sun. They have left out of the picture, as some realists have mentioned, such aspects as the the Mooney case, or strikes or lynchings."[4]

In addition to some scornful critics, some of the public—for whom the artists created their frescoes in the first place—did not deal very kindly with the art. After twenty-three years the frescoes had been so badly vandalized that in 1957 San Francisco artist Joseph Rowland offered to replace them with redwood-and-aluminum panels, like those he created for the World Trade Center, for $50,000. Luckily for the murals, Park Commissioner Francis Herz declined Rowland's offer, seeking instead "an inexpensive restoration and possibly a mar-proof coating to protect the paintings."

Coit Tower Closed—Again

By 1960 the vandalism had created a large arabesque of exposed white plaster showing through the paint pigments of the frescoes. The Recreation and Park Department, under whose jurisdiction the Tower remains to this day, ordered locked glass doors installed to keep the public out of the first floor corridor and locked the door of the stairway leading to the second floor. Dorothy Puccinelli Craveth, a local artist, began a gentle restoration of the vandalized portions of the paintings, engaging whenever possible the original artists for the touching up. In 1975 another local artist, Emmy Lou Packard, restored portions of the art that had been damaged by water seepage, plaster cracking, scratches, and flecked paint. She also removed a forty-year accumulation of cigarette smoke film on the lobby oil panels. (The lobby had remained open to provide access to the observation deck elevator.)

For seventeen years the public peeked through exterior windows to catch a glimpse of the art treasures behind the locked glass doors. The Recreation and Park Department wanted to open the Tower to the public again, but wondered how to protect the frescoes from people whose fingers itched to compete with the artists. Commissioner Herz's idea of a "mar-proof coating" did not appeal to the artists. They were waiting to see the formation of the traditional "crystal" or marbleizing of the chemicals on the surface of exposed frescoes, as has occurred in the ancient Egyptian, Roman, and Florentine murals. Edith Hamlin, one of the second floor artists, favored the idea of guards to patrol the area and railings to serve as security against vandalism. Emmy Lou Packard prepared a plan for such protection, suggesting in addition a closed circuit TV surveillance system.

Park Commissioner Francis Herz pointing out graffiti scratched on original Coit Tower art

Coit Tower Reopened

At last, in 1977, public interest caused the Recreation and Park Department to open the doors for two hours a day, later extended, under guarded supervision. Paul Yuke, former Business Manager of the Department, was instrumental in this reopening. Packard suggested a large guest book for the public, which was well used.

Writing about the reopening of the lower floor murals on May 4, 1977, San Francisco *Chronicle* reporter Peter Kuehl focused on the presence of the only two master artists to attend the ceremony, Suzanne Scheuer and Bernard Zakheim, both eighty years old by now. Gone is the purple-prose-which-saw-red of the 1930s. Kuehl concluded his report: "Most of the frescoes reflect the tough depression times, showing men and women at hard labor. The eyes stare straight ahead and there is little joy in the faces."

Presently, plans are under discussion for applying a protective coating to the outside walls of the Tower, to prevent erosion and to protect the interior murals from additional water damage.

Summing Up: A Historian's View

Historical objectivity is nearly impossible *in medias res.* With the benefit of hindsight, a new generation can

Dorothy Puccinelli Cravath gently restoring a section of Industries of California, 1960; Stackpole painted fellow artist William Hesthal in checkered shirt.

Emmy Lou Packard cleaning elevator lobby panel, with assistance from janitor, Mr. Wilson, and caretaker, Dorothy Ellis, 1975

Water damage to City Life

survey with detachment the progress of the past. In 1976, in connection with a retrospective exhibit called "New Deal Art" in the University of Santa Clara's de Saisset Gallery, historian Steven Gelber wrote an article called "The Irony of San Francisco's 'Commie Art.'" Commenting on the artistic isolation of California, "a cultural backwater," he noted that in the 1930s the American art scene nationally had two schools. The first was Regionalism, which glorified rural America in clearcut representational terms, particularly shunning the European avant-garde. The second was Social Realism, an often critical view of American society and usually in an urban perspective. Despite the three-thousand-mile distance from the East Coast, both schools exist at Coit Tower. As McKinzie pointed out in *A New Deal for Artists*, both approaches avoid-

Bernard B. Zakheim, with daughter Masha Zakheim Jewett and granddaughters; Zakheim's daughter Ruth appears in the mural, dressed in a middy blouse.

ed the potential shocks to an uninformed public of "cubism, futurism, and all forms of modernism." For the most part, the artists, the national administration, and the local sponsors, who "matched" federal support, usually shared the same philosophy: "Paint what is right with America."

Thus it seems that the Coit Tower Four whose words and symbols had caused such a stir were the exception rather than the rule. In contrast to those critics who saw only grim Depression figures in the iconography of Coit Tower, Gelber maintained that there was a "nearly unanimous refusal to paint the Depression," a refusal that was a "statement of faith in the American system. To the painters the Depression was an anomaly. It should not have been there, and by not painting it the artists were expressing their support of the American socio-economic system."[5] In fact, he said, the artists even "bent over backwards to avoid painting propaganda"—no heroic portraits of officials and rarely any reference to relief programs.

However, as Gelber told it, ironically the art turned out to be propaganda after all—propaganda glorifying the New Deal and its message of promised plenty and hope for the future. The artists did not challenge, question, or criticize the system that fed them. "They were merely expressing their genuine support of a system that was paying them money to paint in the middle of the Depression."

In retrospect it would seem that the criticisms of the 1930s, though occasionally scathing, produced the most colorful rhetoric. It wasn't until later years that writers applied such terms as "grim," "depressed," "grotesque," and "little joy."

Despite the publicity given to the works mentioned, the vast majority of art at Coit Tower shows everyday life without incident. The farmers, the cowboy, the lawyers, the stockbroker, the inventor, the mill and steel workers go about their normal tasks wearing neutral if not joyous expressions. The fashionable population of Powell Street does not suggest a revolution tomorrow. Upstairs the collegians at sport, the campers, the outdoor sportsmen, the people in the park, and the overview of a family at work and at play all suggest a "domestic tranquility." Since these aspects did not make headlines or sensational copy, reporters ignored them.

A careful viewer of the murals in Coit Tower will be rewarded with many delightful vignettes and even "in jokes" among the artists. Although Howard's industrial workers look stern and serious, one of his farmers carries a tobacco sack in his pocket which has the artist's name on the circular label under the familiar Bull Durham logo. Although there is the National Recovery Administration eagle insignia on a lug of oranges in the orchard, the women picking flowers in Albro's mural could be attired for a garden party. Although the grass of disuse grows among the railroad ties in Hestal's *Railroad and Shipping*, he has left behind a promising little oilcan on the shelf in his window alcove. Although the agricultural workers are laboring in Boynton's *Animal Force*, a farmer throws a loving arm around the neck of his horse. Although one reader reaches for *Das Kapital* in Zakheim's library, another reads a book called *Weird Spirit*. Although the stock market chart shows a startling downward plunge in George Harris's stock market scene, the books on the shelves of his law library sport unexpected titles like *The Law of Averages* and *The Laws of Fresco Painting, 1934*. Upstairs, Terada's polo players suggest a Persian miniature writ large, and Cunningham's picnickers lunch in front of trees that are reminiscent of a Flemish tapestry.

The eagle symbol of the National Recovery Act, detail from California, M. Albro

It is a matter of historical record that the Coit Tower art project was the prototype for the decade of New Deal art that followed, 1933–43, halted finally by World War II. Utilizing carefully selected artistic talent, the project provided an iconography of the "American Scene" for the largest of all the art programs of that time, the Works Progress Administration's Federal Art Project (WPA-FAP) which followed a year after the PWAP. The themes of agriculture, education, urban and rural life, social protest, and New Deal idealism established at Coit Tower were to become the subsequent subjects of those same artists and of others who took up paintbrushes and sculptors' tools under further government-sponsored art programs throughout the nation. It was to be a reaffirmation of the ideology of the Roosevelt administration, looking for a better life during the economic Depression of the 1930s. Dr. Belisario Contreras, historian of New Deal art, has suggested that despite the controversies, here was hope that rather than a nightmare of shattered illusions the American Dream could be a viable reality.

For those who would hear it, there is a strong lyrical note that sings out high and bright above the bass tones of factual Social Realism at Coit Tower.

The promise of a well-oiled future, detail from Railroad and Shipping, *W. Hesthal*

PART II:
THE ART, A WALKING GUIDE

THE first-time visitor to Coit Tower often thinks that one artist painted all the murals. This unity exists because most of the artists utilized Mexican muralist Diego Rivera's intense colors, rounded forms, two-dimensional overlappings, standardized scale, and earthen color palette. The murals depict a common theme, "Aspects of Life in California, 1934." Most important, the fresco technique itself is a binding, cohesive force in these works of art.

A similar unity exists among the oil murals in the elevator lobby. Each is an accurate geographical "window" to the 1930s San Francisco Bay scene: East Bay hills and cities; North Bay hills and Alcatraz Island; and to the south, Santa Clara Valley. A map above the original art-deco elevator identifies the panorama.

Just as the lobby presents a microcosmic view of the past, the top of the Tower, with its eight portals in a belvedere, provides today's viewer with the macrocosmic landscape of the 1980s.

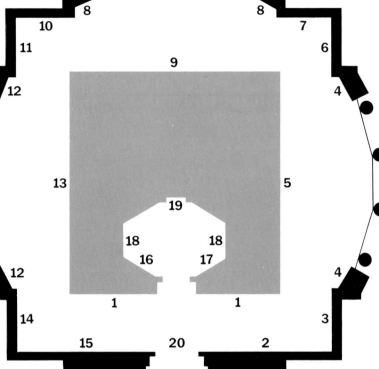

Coit Tower Floor Plan

1. *Animal Force and Machine Force* by Ray Boynton
2. *California Industrial Scenes* by John Langley Howard
3. *Railroad and Shipping* by William Hesthal
4. *Surveyor* and *Steelworker* by Clifford Wight
5. *Industries of California* by Ralph Stackpole
6. *Newsgathering* by Suzanne Scheuer
7. *Library* by Bernard B. Zakheim
8. *Stockbroker* and *Scientist-Inventor* by Mallette Dean
9. *City Life* by Victor Arnautoff
10. *Banking and Law* by George Harris
11. *Department Store* by Frede Vidar
12. *Farmer* and *Cowboy* by Clifford Wight
13. *California* by Maxine Albro
14. *Meat Industry* by Ray Bertrand
15. *California Agricultural Industry* by Gordon Langdon
16. *San Francisco Bay, East* by Otis Oldfield
17. *San Francisco Bay, North* by Jose Moya del Pino
18. *Bay Area Hills* by Rinaldo Cuneo
19. *Seabirds* and *Bay Area Map* by Otis Oldfield
20. *Power* by Fred Olmsted, Jr.

The following murals are open to the public by special arrangement:

21. *Powell Street* by Lucien Labaudt
22. *Collegiate Sports* by Parker Hall
23. *Sports* by Edward Terada
24. *Children at Play* by Ralph Chesse
25. *Hunting in California* by Edith Hamlin
26. *Outdoor Life* by Ben F. Cunningham
27. *Home Life* by Jane Berlandina

1. *Animal Force and Machine Force*
Ray Boynton / fresco / 10 feet by 36 feet

This strategically placed fresco serves several important functions at Coit Tower. First, it is the visitor's introduction to the artwork. Second, it contains a balance of the two major themes, the rural and industrial/urban scenes of California, 1934. And finally, it is the counterpart of the metropolitan panel by Victor Arnautoff (9). Boynton was the "dean of fresco painters," having pioneered that medium in a private home in California in 1917. He was also a senior member of the art faculty at the University of California at Berkeley, and thus advisor and mentor to many other artists.

In his wall, an alcove at far left contains a DAR bronze plaque commemorating the inner signal station on Telegraph Hill (1849) and the first western telegraph station (1853). He decorated the area around it with rocks and cacti, then placed a seated boy, hands clasped around his knees, looking at a book whose pages show the date of Coit Tower (1933) and of the Public Works of Art Project (1934).

The left-hand portion of Boynton's fresco portrays animal power in agriculture, with two horses pulling a fish net, a bubbly child's tree at a vertical river, haystacks, fields, a dairy barn, and a horse against which a farmhand, a portrait of fellow artist Gordon Langdon (15), fondly leans. The simplistic lack of perspective implies the innocence of the Regionalistic portrayal of farm life. Over the the entrance to the elevator lobby

NO SMOKING

Boynton paints soulful eyes (Tower workmen called the image "Old Man Weather") gazing over a quarter-moon at left, connected by clouds to a full sun at right. (These symbols may have Masonic significance.) Underneath is an eagle, perched mid-air, flanked by two birds. Decorating the arched doorway are a girl, the artist's wife Kathleen Boynton, harvesting grapes, and a boy pruning grapevines. Symbolizing machine force, a train runs from the sun towards a man controlling the power of a dam (Boynton ignores the "architectural accident" of an art-deco lighting fixture in the middle of it), while water flows toward a hydroelectric plant, and a large pulley runs out of the picture at the bottom. While a surveyor makes notes in his log, a steam shovel scoops rocks at the far right, with derricks in the background. A visor-capped man operates a drill, his face partially eclipsed, his gloved hands delicately clutching the handle of the pneumatic drill. In sum, in *Animal Force* man seeks food (survival); in *Machine Force*, wealth (power).

2. *California Industrial Scenes*
John Langley Howard / fresco / 10 feet by 24 feet

To balance the agricultural scenes at Coit Tower, Howard portrays industry, including construction, oil-well drilling, and mining. Son of prominent Bay Area architect John Galen Howard, this artist portrays a politically sensitive scene using the force of labor as Mexican muralist Siqueiros rather than Rivera might have presented it. There is a contrast between the somewhat abstractly painted solemn, determined workers demonstrating on May Day, a traditional international labor holiday, and the carefully articulated tools of work in the foreground beneath the window alcove. There are several small groups that blend together to create a montage of rocks, gold panning, dredging, growing plants, large rectangular roofs, and a hydroelectric plant. An angry woman washes clothes by hand in the effluence of the powerful Shasta Dam, while an elderly woman saws a log by hand which, by suggestion, might well have been cut by utilizing some of that same electric power. Another ironic pictorial comment is the migrant family posed near the tent with their broken-down Model-T Ford, with a wheel lying in the dust, next to a group of affluent observers in furs and suits with their liveried chauffeur and a streamlined Chrysler Air-Flow Engine limousine. The artist mingles physical proportions: on the train trestle is a tiny hobo with a sack and pole, while in the foreground, in human scale, a lunch-break worker leans against a culvert next to a cat with

kittens. On the ground are newspapers with headlines like "Relief Rolls Reach New All Time Peak" and "'I'm a Tough Guy,' Franklin Roosevelt warns Congress; 'I learned a lot from the barracudas and sharks,' Roosevelt tells crowd at Station." Not only does Howard physically portray the industrial scene; he also conveys a powerful social and political message through his juxtaposition of strong visual images typical of the Social Realist style of the time.

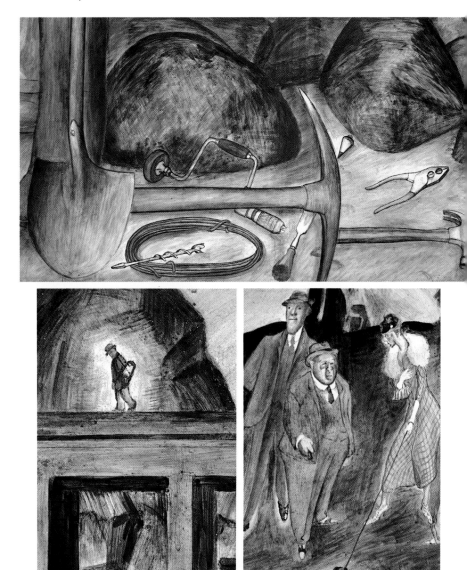

3. *Railroad and Shipping*
William Hesthal / fresco / 10 feet by 10 feet

Intent on showing the effects of the New Deal on the stagnant economy of the 1930s, this artist presents the symbols of the transportation of commerce: train and boat. At left center a train is about to leave on a track which workers are clearing of the weeds of disuse. On the other side is the hull of a boat, in front of which is a seated signalman peering around the corner, pipe in mouth, to see a worker at left (probably local sculptor David Slivka). Behind the boat is the Third Street bridge at China Basin, newly completed in 1933. Overhead, a railroad shafts into the viewer's field, a departure from Diego Rivera's rule of two-dimensionality in wall paintings. (The artist later attributed this violation of the Rivera rubric to "youthful rebellion against the rules!") Utilizing the window alcove as a shelf, Hestal has left an oilcan behind, suggesting that the sluggish transportation industry in the Depression might be made to run again with a little lubrication (perhaps from the government-sponsored New Deal art project). The color tones here are dark and somber, suggesting cloudy weather in which unemployed workers are resigned to patient waiting for some activity on wharf and track, land and sea.

4. *Surveyor* and *Steelworker*
Clifford Wight / frescoes / each 10 feet by 4 feet

As an industrial counterbalance to Wight's two agricultural
workers on the east wall (12) are these two industrial icon figures on the west wall: a surveyor stands solid, surveyor's level
poised, maps in hand, looking at an impassive steelworker opposite him whose wrenches hang at his side, reaching from
waist to knee. The controversial part of this fresco is gone.
Junius Cravens (San Francisco *News*, July 1934) described
Wight's intention of symbolizing alternative social systems

available at that time: "Over the central window he stretched a bridge, at the center of which is a circle containing the Blue Eagle of the NRA. Over the right-hand window he stretched a segment of chain; in the circle in this case appears the legend, 'In God We Trust'—symbolizing the American dollar, or . . . Capitalism. Over the left-hand window he placed a section of woven cable and a circle framing a hammer, a sickle, and the legend 'United Workers of the World,' in short, Communism." The slogan and the symbols disappeared before the Tower was opened to the public in 1934.

5. *Industries of California*
Ralph Stackpole / fresco / 10 feet by 36 feet

Sculptor Ralph Stackpole painted this synthesis of industrial activities in California to counterbalance the agricultural panel by Maxine Albro (13). Noted usually for his three-dimensional works, he here creates large modeled shapes in the industrial pipes, barrels, storage tanks, and machinery characterized by the convoluted plastic forms reminiscent of Rivera's murals.

In contrast to the rounded bulges of the large background mechanisms, the human figures have a flat, two-dimensional pencil-sketch quality as the chemists (Tom Lehman, a local artist, pours chemicals into a retort, while checker-shirted William Hesthal [3] bends over a table, notebook in hand) go about their work. The women workers in uniforms and hairnets (some identifiable, like Helen Clement Mills, second right in the other panel) pack food, and the men stand at an assembly line near sacks of sugar labeled with the NRA eagle. Tom Hayes, one of George Harris's "authors" in the law library panel (10), assisted Stackpole. In keeping with the brown-grey tones of the subject matter, the artist chose a rather subdued palette.

6. *Newsgathering*
Suzanne Scheuer / fresco / 10 feet by 10 feet

Suitably adjacent to the library panel, this extension of the printed word demonstrates the submission of a news item to a white-haired editor (art patron William Gerstle), to the process of printing it in the newspaper, to the final edition sold on the street. The boy is probably Peter Stackpole, son of artist Ralph Stackpole (5) and later an important photographer of the building of the two San Francisco bridges. Though the boy hawks the .San Francisco *Gazette*, which never existed, on the window ledge there is a replica of the front page of the San Francisco *Chronicle*. The artist has written on it: "Artists Finish Coit Tower Murals, April 1934; Albro, Arnautoff, Boynton, Stackpole, Langdon, Howard, Daum [her assistant]." The border design around the window shows the color process used to produce a comic strip (in this case "Moon Mullins") from start to finish.

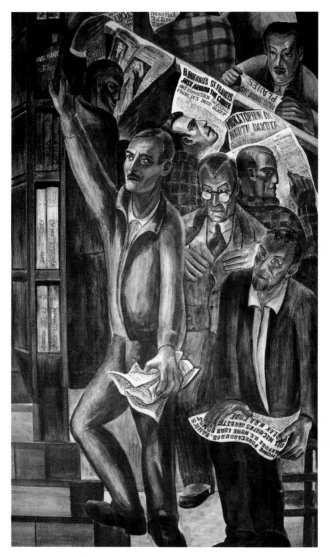

7. *Library*
Bernard B. Zakheim / fresco / 10 feet by 10 feet

This interior of a public library balances the law library by Harris at far left. Like other artists, Zakheim peopled his scene (public library reading and periodical rooms) with portraits, including his young daughter Ruth (in a middy blouse); his assistant Shirley Staschen Triest (transformed into a boy); Coit Tower caretaker VFW Col. William Brady reading a book entitled *Weird Spirit* (did he haunt the Tower at night?); at the table, a former assistant, Julia Hamberg Rogers, next to a portrait of the artist reading a book in Hebrew; and a blind boy "fingering" a book in Braille. In the periodical room, fellow artist Ralph Stackpole (5) reads a headline concerning the destruction of the Rivera mural at Rockefeller Center in New York in 1933; local sculptor Beniamino Bufano reads, "B. Bufano's St.

Francis Just Around the Corner; Art Commission Awakens from Its Deep Sleep;"—all subjects of current interest at the time. Right center, Col. Harold Mack (on the Washington-appointed supervisory committee of the PWAP) with thumbs in his vest armholes, looks on, while fellow artist John Langley Howard (2) holds a crumpled newspaper while reaching for Marx's *Das Kapital* from a library shelf. Joseph Danysh, later Federal Art Project director, holds a paper about mortgage foreclosures; at lower right is an eccentric friend, Louie Kramer. Above the window are three books lying on their sides in the central stack; their Hebrew letters spell out their contents: *Torah* (Scriptures), *Prophets*, and *Wisdom Literature*, books of the Old Testament. His "gun-slit" window invites the viewer up the steps into the library containing classical authors like Defoe, Smollett, Fielding, Swift, and Oscar Wilde, as well as writers of the 1930s like Dos Passos, Jeffers, Stuart Chase, and Kenneth Rexroth, the young poet who supplied most of the authors' names, here shown on the library ladder. The boy at the left reads a comic strip by BBZ, the artist, outstanding here for his use of intensely rich, dark colors.

8. *Stockbroker* and *Scientist-Inventor*

Mallette (Harold) Dean / two fresco panels
each 10 feet by 4 feet

The stockbroker at left (perhaps A.P. Giannini, founder of the Bank of America) with the ticker tape and telephone carries on the banking theme from the Harris mural (10). He seems dignified but worried, in contrast with the scientist-inventor on the other side of the large south window, who holds a radio part and a scroll as he stands near a mini-picture of the James Lick Observatory on Mount Hamilton, San Jose, California. The observatory is cleverly worked around the "architectural accident" of a light switch plate, which serves as a door to the observatory.

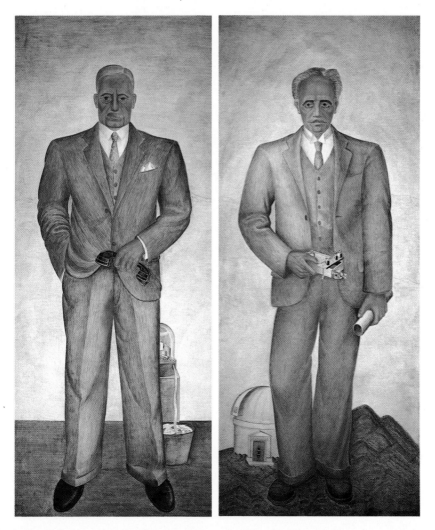

9. *City Life*
Victor Arnautoff / fresco / 10 feet by 36 feet

A favorite of visitors, this busy urban scene is a pastiche of downtown San Francisco locations, characterized by the cross-streets Montgomery and Washington, located in the financial district, from which it is actually impossible to see the California Palace of the Legion of Honor museum in Lincoln Park, shown at upper right near a support beam. Workmen, traffic rushing by, an auto accident, a holdup, a razor vendor, and a fire ladder truck labeled No. 5 (symbolizing Lillie Hitchcock Coit's association with Knickerbocker Engine No. 5 of the Volunteer Fire Department in the 1860s) mesh together with a cluttered newspaper stand (through which a door is cut). Periodicals like the leftist *New Masses* and *Daily Worker,* and *Time, Argonaut,* and *Screenplay* (with Mae West on the cover) appear on its racks. Conspicuous by its absence is the San Francisco *Chronicle,* though three other dailies of that time are evident. (That omission caused great consternation in the local press.) Near the magazines are a self-portrait, with the artist wearing a fur-collared coat, and a banker reading the New York stock returns. In the background are the City Hall, Main Library, and the Stock Exchange building (with Ralph Stackpole's sculpture outside it). Charlie Chaplin peers out of a sign announcing his movie *City Lights* (not the famous San Francisco bookstore,

which came a generation later). A produce-market scene at far right thematically connects with the agricultural Albro fresco (13) around the corner from it to the right, while the men doing industrial work at left reflect the Stackpole mural (5) around the left corner. A large, bland, green U.S. mailbox in the foreground placidly contrasts with the frantic activity around it, orchestrated by the static policeman directing traffic.

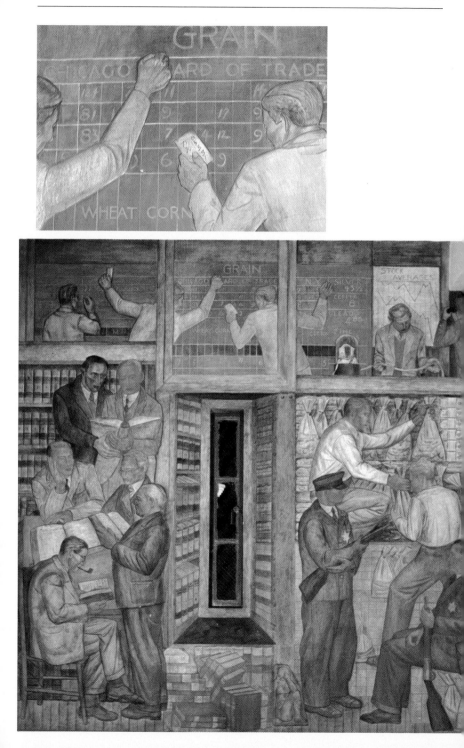

10. *Banking and Law*
George Harris / fresco / 10 feet by 10 feet

The worlds of finance and law are represented here by a Federal Reserve Bank, the Stock Exchange (above), and a law library, with appropriate readers and guardians. The library at left makes fascinating reading. The titles begin soberly enough, with law books titled *Civil, Penal, Political,* and *Moral Codes.* But suddenly there are books by Harris entitled *Law or Justice, Law of Averages, Laws of Fresco Painting, 1934,* and some satirizing fellow artists: *Counterfeiting* by Hesthal; *Laws on Seduction* by Herr Vidar; *Married Women* by Zakheim; *Martial Law* by Brady (the VFW caretaker who watched the project by day and lived in the Tower's apartment on the second floor at night); *Prohibition—Volstead Laws* by Cuneo; books called *Rape, Mayhem,* and *Vagrancy* by "Professor" Bertrand (14); *Art and Artists* by Master Thomas Hayes (assistant to several artists); and tucked into a corner, a joke unto itself, *Unwritten Laws* by Judge Lynch. Elsewhere, an open book shows illegible names under a list of lawyers, but on the opposite page titled "Etc." are listed "Darrow, C., Holmes, Lincoln, A." The man at left holding a pipe is probably William Gerstle, a local patron of the arts. The curly-headed blond boy is Fred Olmsted, Jr. (20), assistant to John Langley Howard (2) and later an artist in the Federal Art Project. In contrast with the scholars reading the law books is the right-hand scene: guards with guns protecting the large money bags at the bank—force versus dispassionate law. At the top, between the two, several clerks write figures on the stock market exchange boards, while the stocks take an alarming downward plunge.

MILK
Today's Menu
1 Soup 5
2 Chili Con Carne 15
3 Tamale
4 Spaghetti
5 Roast Beef
6 Corned Beef
7 Sliced
8

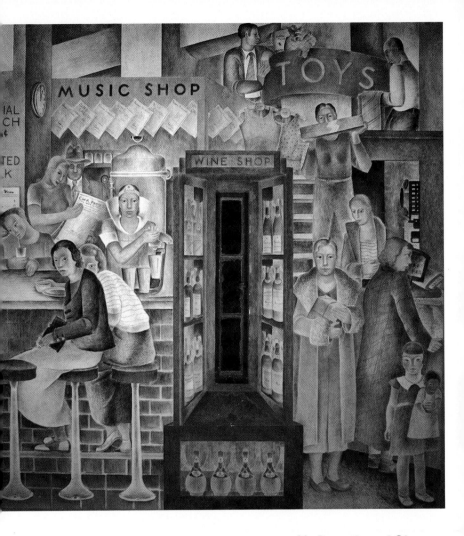

11. *Department Store*
Frede Vidar / fresco / 10 feet by 10 feet

Here is the interior of a typical 1930s department store, even to the details of a soda fountain, a wine shop in the window alcove (which contains only domestic vintages!), fabric counter, clothing departments, a toy shop with dolls of comic-strip characters Barney Google and Sparkplug, customers, and salespeople. At the lunch counter a waitress wears a cap with a Star of David (a surprising Jewish symbol, as Frede Vidar frequently expressed pro-Nazi sympathies in 1934, and even scratched a swastika on the whitewashed windowpane when he worked on the project); two dispirited young women (one might be Hebe Daum, later the wife of Peter Stackpole [5]) sit in front of a menu offering a special lunch for 25 cents, soup for 5

cents, and chile con carne for 15 cents. (One must remember, however, that most of the master artists on the PWAP project at Coit Tower were receiving approximately one dollar an hour.) In the background are copies of music of the day: Bing Crosby alternates with *Roman Scandals* by Irving Berlin. A newspaper dated February 1934 headlines CWA (Civil Works Administration, the government agency authorizing the PWAP, under whose auspices the Coit Tower project existed); further down on that same page is a faint likeness of Hitler, with his name barely legible in a newspaper caption.

12. *Farmer* and *Cowboy*
Clifford Wight / two fresco panels / each 10 feet by 4 feet

These two single figures pose almost like Byzantine icons on either side of a large window representing two dominant strands of California country life: the cowboy herding cattle and the farmer tending crops. The Will Rogers–style cowboy might be a self-portrait in the manner of Cezanne, with its face full of geometric planes. The farmer could be Ralph Stackpole, San Francisco sculptor (5). The artist camouflaged the "architectural accident" of a light switch in the trouser leg of the farmer's overalls.

13. *California*
Maxine Albro / fresco / 10 feet by 42 feet

In this well-balanced scene of California's agricultural life, 1934, the artist shows the riches reaped from the soil: at left are workers in the flower industry wearing what were at that time called "beach pajamas." Prominent among them, holding the calla lilies, is Helen Clement Mills, assistant to Gordon Langdon (15). At the top of the mural are seasonal scenes—a bright summer sun over a dairy, snow on wintery Mt. Shasta, springtime almond orchards in bloom, and at far right, autumnal rains. At right are the symbols of the state's vineyards and wineries of Sonoma and Napa Valleys; "gentlemen farmers" are actual portraits of the artist's friends, such as fellow artists

Ralph Stackpole (in the checkered shirt) and her husband,
fellow artist Parker Hall, (22), by the trays of apricots. Albro
entices the viewer to ignore the door in the center (originally
painted a bright blue) by leading the eye above it to look down
a row of trees in a modified vanishing point. The NRA eagle on
the lugs of oranges is the only sign that this bucolic scene exists
in the middle of the Great Depression of the 1930s.

14. *Meat Industry*
Ray Bertrand / fresco / 10 feet by 10 feet

Related to the animal motif of its neighbor, the dairy industry (15), this panel illustrates meat packing, from the hanging and cleaning of pigs through the processing of hams. A large butchered hog dominates the left-hand portion, with a rubber-booted worker singeing the skin with a large flame. Bertrand's alcove becomes a smokehouse hung with sausages draped over the coiled smoke-pipes. An overhead pulley system draws the viewer's attention to the hog carcasses in the foreground, directing the eye to wrapped hams at right, where a woman works a spring scale, her graceful hand resting lightly on a ham; in the foreground sit wooden lugs and barrels, giving a cubistic definition to the composition. The subtle colors of flesh, tans, greys, and greens contrast with the diagonally opposite (13) oranges, purples, and bright greens of Albro's bountiful harvest.

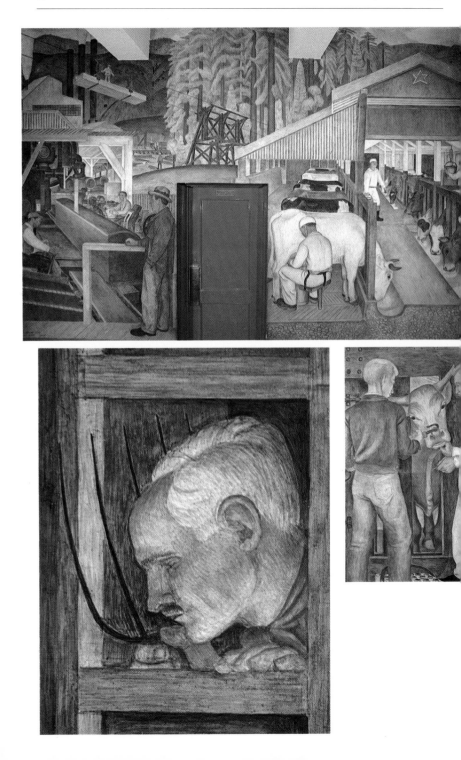

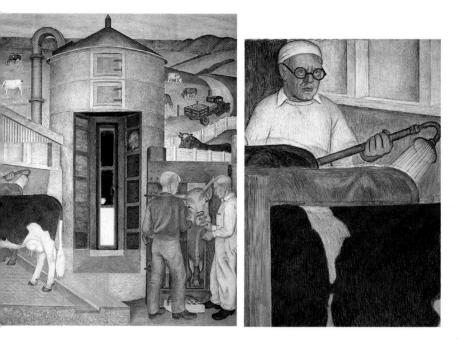

15. *California Agricultural Industry*
Gordon Langdon / fresco / 10 feet by 27 feet

Connected naturally by position and subject matter to Howard's mural (2), Langdon's painting shows the "agri-business" of timber and dairy. Assisted by Helen Clement Mills (13), Langdon extends the theme by showing a lumber mill, forests, and a dairy barn, with a five-pointed star at the roof peak, housing cows being milked and groomed. Fellow artist Lucien Labaudt (21) is showering and scrubbing a cow. The window alcove has become the interior of a silo, with a farmer (fellow artist John Langley Howard) holding a pitchfork as he peeks through a painted window. In the foreground fellow artist Fred Olmsted, Jr., and assistant Tom Hayes are working with cattle, a box of medicines at their side. In the distance one sees a dairy truck, more forest, then sky—as if to suggest the infinite riches of agricultural California. One is conscious of Langdon's rounded forms—the cattle, the silo, pipes, and small pebbles in the foreground, which show a vertical cross-section of the dairy floor, and serve as a visual link with Howard's companion mural at left.

16. *San Francisco Bay*
Otis Oldfield / oil on canvas in a recessed lunette
9 feet by 54 inches

Unlike the frescoes, which had to be painted on location, this oil on canvas as well as the others in the lobby were completed in the artists' studios and then installed as finished works. From his Telegraph Hill studio, the artist, Otis Oldfield, could see the waterfront and bay all the way to Berkeley. His two young daughters, Rhonda and Jayne, in the lower right-hand corner, look down at boat traffic and the busy waterfront. There were no bridges on the bay in 1934; one sees the harbor, a lighthouse on Yerba Buena Island (which would later "anchor" the central section of the Bay Bridge; Treasure Island had not yet been built for the Golden Gate International Exposition of 1939–40). Bright white steamboats float on the grey water, soft brown hills loom against grey skies—all in muted colors which reflect the typical San Francisco foggy summer. A faint campanile in the East Bay marks the University of California campus. Were a hole knocked through the wall on which the painting now hangs, one could still see that same view from Coit Tower.

17. *San Francisco Bay, North*
Jose Moya del Pino / oil on canvas in a recessed lunette
9 feet by 54 inches

A companion piece to 16, this scene of another part of the bay
matches it in medium, scale, and outlook. An observer (Moya
del Pino himself) watches fellow artist Otis Oldfield (16), wearing his familiar beret, at work as he sketches the northern Embarcadero below him, with boats and sailboats in the bay, and
the uninhabited Marin hills in the distance. Alcatraz Prison is on
the island in the middle of the bay, with factories in left foreground sporting tall, man-shaped chimneys. As in the case of
Oldfield's painting, were the wall transparent the viewer
would still have the same prospect looking north.

18. *Bay Area Hills*
Rinaldo Cuneo / oil on canvas in recessed lunettes
each 9 feet by 54 inches

This pair of canvases depicts the rich farmlands of the Santa Clara Valley and the rounded brownish hills of the East Bay. The artist has massed blossoming trees, vineyards, a man walking with a hoe—all in tones of grey, brown, and subtle green. In the twin painting a man driving a tractor occupies a foreground spot, set against planted green areas, brown fields, small farms and buildings, large hills looming almost to the top of the canvas, and grey skies.

19. *Seabirds* and *Bay Area Map*
Otis Oldfield / oil on canvas in lunettes over doorways

In addition to 16, Oldfield also decorated the two small semi-circular arches over doors in the elevator lobby with bird scenes of native sea gulls and pelicans. To complete the interior he painted a stylized map of the San Francisco Bay Area as the background for the elevator floor-indicator, whose pointer forms a compass arm, superimposed on the water-land swirls of blue, brown, and beige to represent the San Francisco Peninsula, the Marin headlands, various islands, and in the foreground, the East Bay flats where the Sacramento and San Joaquin Rivers empty into the Bay. Preferring oil on canvas to fresco, Oldfield, Moya del Pino, and Cuneo treated color, texture, scale, and subject matter quite differently from the manner of the frescoists. However, these paintings serve as a quiet transition to the vibrant murals which lead the viewer up the staircase to the second floor of Coit Tower.

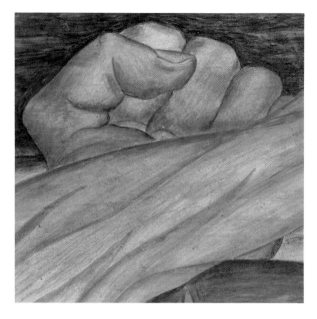

20. *Power*
Fred Olmsted, Jr., / fresco / 3 feet by 3 feet

Serving as a transition between the two industrial scenes (2 and 15) on either side of it, this work is "framed" by a representation of a mechanical device on the left which "supports" the ceiling beam above it and a sawed-off tree stump under the beam at right. Both of these symbolize the panels for which this section is a link. In the center is a powerful clenched fist (representing labor?) which bursts through a bolt of lightning.

21. *Powell Street*
Lucien Labaudt / two fresco panels / each 6 feet by 32 feet

Covering the greatest wall space in the Tower, Labaudt's two busy sides of Powell Street in 1934 flow up each side of the curved stairway, with a connecting stretch over the doorway below. Beginning at Market Street at the bottom of the stairs, these scenes show crowds, buildings, and activities typical of the urban expanse. Because they are so large and so rich in detail, a close study of these murals rewards the viewer with a graphic picture; one recognizes geographic landmarks like the Lincoln Market (now gone), architect Timothy Pflueger's art-deco 450 Sutter Medical and Dental Building (1928), the cable car kiosk at the top of California and Powell Streets, various

hotels and restaurants, including the old Pig 'n' Whistle (long since gone), the Bank of America at the foot of Powell Street by Hallidie Plaza today, and Lucien Labaudt's studio called "The California School of Design," here initialed "LL" (also gone). There are cable cars, billboards advertising Chesterfield cigarettes, Mayor Rossi's name on a headline, a basket of flowers tagged "Wishing You a Happy Easter, 1934," and the only other black man in Coit Tower (besides the worker in Howard's fresco [2]), a bellhop carrying suitcases with European travel stickers. Labaudt also portrays the only Oriental face in the Tower (probably fellow artist Edward Terada [23]), here an industrious-looking student carrying an architect's portfolio at the top of the stairs at right.

Almost every figure in the mural can be identified: at the foot of the stairs to the left is Labaudt's wife Marcelle Lapegue Labaudt, with dark wavy hair; next to her is a group of PWAP representatives looking at a map marked "PWAP" in mirror-image—Edward Bruce, national PWAP Director; Eleanor Roosevelt; L.W. Roberts, U.S. Secretary of the Treasury; local commercial artist Charles Stafford Duncan (wearing round glasses); and Forbes Watson, PWAP Technical Director. Near this group are Helen Clement Mills in a beret; fedora-hatted Gottardo Piazzoni (painter of large oil murals in the Main Library at Civic Center); the three Bruton sisters (also local artists); Ralph Stackpole and his wife Ginette with their son Francis; Mrs. Otis Oldfield and her two daughters; Otis Oldfield higher up on the wall in his French beret; a self-portrait of Labaudt in profile, wearing glasses; fellow artists Victor Arnautoff (9) and Rinaldo Cuneo (18) with cigarette in a holder; architect Timothy Pflueger, half hidden by a mounted policeman; and, at the top of the stairs at left, Fay (wearing a red bow) and Farwell Taylor, also artists. At the base of the stairs on the right-hand side, Moya del Pino (17) holds his baby daughter; Jane Berlandina (27) wears a tie; bearded author Col. Erskine Scott Wood is part of the crowd; and farther up, Mme Labaudt appears a second time, here in fashionable blue cap with match-

ing wide-collared coat. (Labaudt gave his designer's attention
to the attire of his figures, dressing them beautifully in the styles
of the day.) Artist Parker Hall (22) carries a drafting triangle; his
wife, Maxine Albro (13), a rolled-up scroll. At the top of the
stairs are Jane Berlandina again (in a wide-collared green
dress) and local artist Merlin Hardy in brown hat and formal tie.
Many other figures in this fresco tapestry were students at the
design school which Labaudt founded.

Assigned the widest expanse of all, Labaudt filled it
delightfully with his careful attention to fashion design, San
Francisco personalities, and his many friends of all back-
grounds. He used to especially successful advantage the two-
dimensional "stacked" effect of layers of figures, and rich,
glowing colors despite the limited range of the earthen palette
of fresco.

22. *Collegiate Sports*
Parker Hall / fresco / 9 feet by 13 feet

Symbolizing the non-academic activities of college life, 1934, this panel shows the popular team and individual sports of the campus. Over the arch above the stairway a game is in progress between the ancient rivals Stanford and the University of California: a football is about to be tossed back between the straddled legs of a UC player against a background of bleachers whose crowd spells out a giant "S" for Stanford fans. Well-groomed sports participants play badminton, a young man gallanty ties the shoe of a woman tennis player, while a bathing beauty in an intensely blue swimsuit looks on. Archers aim not at their targets but seemingly at nearby baseball players, while three women with a basketball appear to be standing on a baseball diamond base. Scattered small flowers and plants give visual relief to the large forms.

23. *Sports*
Edward Terada / fresco / 9 feet by 10 feet

Above a doorway Terada paints a large sun to serve as a transition between the collegiate sports of fellow artist Parker Hall (22) and Olympic runners with classical Greek profiles; on the next wall are players of golf and polo grouped in postures often associated with Persian miniatures. Although rather stylized, the whole composition flows naturally and gracefully. The musculature of the humans and horses presents rounded, highlighted curves that please the eye, the varied terra cotta shades giving them the quality of fine pottery.

24. *Children at Play*
Ralph Chesse / fresco / 9 feet by 6 feet

In the playground the children jump rope, sail boats, and eat ice cream. In their arrested-in-space activities, they bring to mind Keats' description of the figures on a Grecian urn—just *about* to play. Unlike the overlapped effect of Labaudt's people (21), puppeteer Chesse's children are separated in space. Topping each child's body is a rather serious adult-like head —in the manner of early itinerant American primitive limners who, before the spread of photography, toured large farms with canvases prepared with previously painted bodies awaiting individual face portraits. Chesse achieves unity among these vertical figures by using a winding gravel path to guide the eye from the left edge of the painting downward. Each child forms a unit of one, climbing a slide, playing ball, pulling a small car, and, to one side, submitting to maternal care. Perhaps Chesse's experience in the puppet theater caused him to compose his figures in staccato rather than legato rhythms.

25. *Hunting in California*
Edith Hamlin / fresco / 9 feet by 12 feet

On each side of the elevator door on the second floor two hunters take aim at a graceful curve of iridescent mallard ducks overhead, while three deer inhabit a forest whose large-leafed branches unify this elegant scene by their shapes and the foliage tones of greens, browns, and pale yellows—a sylvan contrast to the earnest hunters on the marsh.

26. *Outdoor Life*
Ben F. Cunningham / fresco / 9 feet by 22 feet

This recreational scene includes picnickers, a piper, a photographer, and others at leisure. Typical of the upstairs frescoes are little separated vignettes: a log splitter; a Matisse-style woman napping with a book nearby, pillowed against a tree; a man with a large camera; a wading boy who ignores his boat in the stream. At a table set for six, four picnickers wait patiently for three slices of bacon that a woman cooks in a pan over a small stove across the stream. A man stands, bucket in hand, pondering the crossing of the running brook. This picnic tableau is set among highly stylized rounded trees whose leaves resemble tapestried jellied wintergreen candies. The flutist entertains a group at left, including a barefoot boy and a seated attentive dog, one forepaw curved under it. At far left, a woman hiker leads a laden donkey down a camping trail, away from the green hills and blue waters. In contrast to the other women who are in skirts, she wears rolled-up jeans and a tight sweater. Such intricate patterns as the tree designs are reminders that Cunningham was a weaver and tapestry designer.

27. *Home Life*
Jane Berlandina / egg tempera
9 feet by 34 feet, in room separate from other murals

Quite different from the fresco and oil media of the other artists in the Tower is the egg-tempera technique of Jane Berlandina, wife of Henry Howard, who was an architect in Arthur Brown, Jr.'s, office, and the designer of Coit Tower. Her teacher was French Post-Impressionist Raoul Dufy, whose style is quite different from that of Diego Rivera, mentor of most of the other

artists. The linear motif outlines life in the kitchen, the living room, and the recreational hall of a home. The color scheme is limited to shades of Indian red, browns, and chartreuse shadows, with white outlines. Each wall has a theme: in the kitchen a mother and two girls make an apple pie. In the living room a bridge game is in progress, with three at the table (one is the artist's husband), and her own self-portrait looking on from behind. A man reads a newspaper while a boy at his feet is absorbed in a book. Above them is a "framed picture" signed by Berlandina. On a third wall beneath a second "framed

picture" (of the hotel in Olema, California) a woman sews a
doll. On the last wall, among a group at a piano, a woman
plays for two ballroom-dancing couples. The doorways sport
painted-on curtains, thematically connecting the other room
decorations, all in russet colors, with chartreuse accents. The
spontaneity of the designs and their "hollow" quality give this
final, isolated room a charming light spirit after the solid frescoes and oils with their more serious subjects on the other walls
at Coit Tower.

APPENDIX:
THE ARTISTS

M A X I N E   A L B R O   was born in Iowa, and studied at the California School of Fine Arts. During the 1920s she studied in Paris, and then in Mexico with Diego Rivera, returning to live in San Francisco. Some of her work figured in a controversy apart from that at Coit Tower: four "portly Roman sybils" that she executed at the Ebell Women's Club in Los Angeles offended some of its members; they rescinded approval of her frescoes which, though intended to last "as long as the concrete of the wall lasted," were destroyed in 1935. Also destroyed was her mosaic of animals over the entrance to Anderson Hall at the University of California Extension in San Francisco. She created fresco decorations for many private homes, including that of Col. Harold Mack in Monterey. Her easel art was popular in local and national museums. Albro was married to fellow artist Parker Hall.

1895–1966
California (13)

V I C T O R   A R N A U T O F F   was a native of Russia, to which he returned during the 1960s after thirty years in the United States. He came to San Francisco via Mexico, where he had assisted Diego Rivera. In San Francisco he attended the California School of Fine Arts, studying with Ralph Stackpole and Edgar Walter. As project director at Coit Tower, he painted a mural as well as supervised the work of fellow artists. Other works include frescoes in the Military Chapel at the Presidio; three fresco lunettes in the Anne Bremer Library of the San Francisco Art Institute; Washington High School lobby; and other locales in the Bay Area. He taught in the art department at Stanford University. During the closing of Coit Tower in 1934, Arnautoff wrote: "I wonder why the windows have been whitewashed—to protect the frescoes from sun-stroke?" He died in March 1979 in retirement in a suburb of Leningrad.

1896–1979
City Life (9)

JANE BERLANDINA came to San Francisco from Nice, France. She studied with Raoul Dufy, and having learned costume design in France, continued this work for the San Francisco Opera Company. Among other projects, she created sets for *Der Rosenkavalier,* starring Lotte Lehmann, and thirty San Francisco scenes for a production of William Saroyan's *Sweeney and the Tree* in 1940. Berlandina exhibited at the Metropolitan Museum in New York as well as in local museums, and was married to architect Henry Howard. Labaudt portrayed Jane Berlandina wearing a sporty necktie at the foot of the stairs in his Powell Street scene at Coit Tower.

1898–1970
Home Life (27)

RAY BERTRAND, a native of San Francisco, was a lithographer as well as an easel artist. He had been a student of Spencer Macky at the California School of Fine Arts, where he later taught lithography. In 1927, he won the Anne Bremer scholarship, enabling him to make "outstanding contributions to the development of the graphic arts of the West" as both an easel artist and lithographer. He was primarily a landscape painter. Reporting on one exhibit, a critic commented that Bertrand used "freezing blues, whites, and greys" in his oils in a "small but icy collection of arctic landscapes." One popular lithograph that he made was "Sierra Fantasy." Fellow artist George Harris painted his name as the "author" of books titled *Rape, Mayhem,* and *Vagrancy* in the "law library" at Coit Tower. In 1942 he won an Abraham Rosenburg Scholarship enabling him to continue his study of color lithography.

1909–ca. 1949
Meat Industry (14)

RAY BOYNTON came from the farms of Iowa, where he had been, among other things, a teamster driving horses. After studying art in Chicago, Boynton came west to make his mark as California's first frescoist. His first fresco appeared in a home in Los Altos in 1917· his later work paralleled but was not derivative of Diego Rivera's in Mexico. While teaching fresco at the California School of Fine Arts, he created the first large-scale mural in a building open to the public: frescoes in a classical mode on the subject of music in the auditorium at Mills College in Oakland. Boynton became a beloved teacher at the University of California in Berkeley, where former student Mary Fabilli remembered, "We learned what to put into a drawing and, mostly, what to leave out." By virtue of his expertise and seniority, he was the "dean of the fresco painters" at Coit Tower, where younger artists sought his expert and freely given advice. During the 1930s Boynton did many sketches of mining scenes in the Mother Lode, and after Coit Tower he painted thirteen lunette murals in tempera for the Modesto post office in 1936. He was a friend of John Steinbeck and Col. Scott Wood, among others, and helped to create the mood which he commended at Coit Tower: "the old cooperative guild spirit with all the artists

1883–1951
*Animal Force and
Machine Force* (1)

working in harmony toward a common end." When in 1976 the Oakland Museum of Art sponsored a memorial monograph about his Mother Lode drawings, twenty-two contributors warmly remembered Ray Boynton.

R A L P H   C H E S S E , born in New Orleans, came to San Francisco to become active among local artists in the early 1930s. A professional puppeteer, he worked mainly in children's theater, and sculptured wood, painted, and consulted in color and design. Knowing Ralph Stackpole, he became part of the Coit Tower project, and was assigned the scene of the children's playground on the second floor. As in the case of John Langley Howard, Chesse's Tower fresco was his first and only painting in that medium. In it he tried to capture the spirit of early itinerant primitive American artists who went from farm to farm with pre-painted canvases whose faces were to be finished with portraits of the actual sitters. Later he worked at the Federal Theater at the Golden Gate Exposition (Treasure Island), 1939–40. During World War II, he made many paintings of the shipyards. Today he lives in Berkeley, California.

b. 1900
Children at Play (24)

R I N A L D O   C U N E O , a native San Franciscan, grew up in the Italian neighborhood of North Beach, where he maintained a studio. In 1910 he began art studies under sculptor Arthur Putnam and artist Gottardo Piazzoni. In 1908 he met Ralph Stackpole to whom he gave his first sculpture commission. After studying at the old Mark Hopkins Art Institute, he went to Paris and London. He taught at the California School of Fine Arts, and though a prolific painter, held few exhibitions and sold few works. He painted competently and quickly as in the case of the oil painting for the Coit Tower lobby; when William Gaw could not join the project, Cuneo painted the second lunette in addition to his own. Harris has "immortalized" him in the "law library" as "author" of Prohibition—Volstead Laws. Cuneo said of his own work: "I love the city and I love the mountains. I have painted still life and portraits, but I prefer landscape. To me there is more life in a mountain than in a human figure." Of his participation at Coit Tower he said, "We all worked in a cooperative spirit and were happy."

1877–1939
Bay Area Hills (18)

B E N   C U N N I N G H A M came to San Francisco in 1924 from Colorado by way of the University of Nevada in Reno, where he studied architecture. He stopped "temporarily" at the California School of Fine Arts, and eventually abandoned architecture. After Coit Tower, he was an assistant art director for the Northern California Federal Art Project. His work at the Tower reflects his tapestry designing experience. Of his art, fellow artist Ralph Chesse said that "Cunningham was a good designer and meticulous draftsman in his decorations." In an article that Cunningham wrote

1904–1977
Outdoor Life (26)

on government funding of the arts for the San Francisco Art Association in 1937, he said that no artist's contribution can be considered relative. "The difference between being able to paint and not being able to paint is absolute. From there on the morale of the artist is of primary importance to his work." He is remembered by his friends as a sensitive, intellectually insightful artist.

MALLETTE (HAROLD) DEAN, one of the most prolific painters of government-sponsored murals in Northern California, was born in Washington. Arriving in San Francisco, he also studied at the California School of Fine Arts. Along with Clifford Wight, Dean painted two icon-like figures in Coit Tower—a stockbroker and a scientist-inventor—demonstrating his own inventiveness by converting a light switch plate on the wall into the door of an astronomical observatory. A furniture designer, decorator of books, and graphic artist, for many years he created labels for the California wine industry. Among his government-sponsored murals is an orchard scene in the Sebastopol post office. He is also represented in the San Francisco Museum of Art and the New York Public Library. He spent his last years in San Rafael, where he died in 1976.

1907–1976
Stockbroker and
Scientist-Inventor (8)

PARKER HALL came from Colorado to attend the California School of Fine Arts. Some of his work is represented at the Library of Congress. He was married to fellow artist Maxine Albro. His Coit Tower mural demonstrates a knowledge of college sports wherein both the University of California and Stanford are represented. Hall lived in Carmel, and preferred to keep his Coit Tower work in the distant past.

1898–1983
Collegiate Sports (22)

EDITH HAMLIN, a native of California, was one of the many students at the California School of Fine Arts who came to work at Coit Tower. She is a woman of many talents and art genres, for besides fresco she has painted on paper, canvas, and gesso. Her work exists in private homes; in post offices in Tracy and Martinez, California; and at Mission High School in San Francisco (1936–37) where her oil-on-canvas murals show "Civilization through the Arts and Crafts as taught the Neophyte Indians by Fathers Danti, Landaeta, and Espi at Mission Delores, 1770–1806" and "Mission San Francisco de Assisi Founded by Palou and Cambon in 1782–91." Later she went to Washington, D.C., to paint two panels in the Department of the Interior building. At Coit Tower her subjects were recreation and outdoor sports—showing duck-hunting, wild geese flying, and graceful deer grazing. She was married to local artist Maynard Dixon, noted for his paintings of the Southwest. She lives in San Francisco.

b. 1902
Hunting in California
(25)

G E O R G E   H A R R I S at twenty-one was among the youngest artists to work at Coit Tower. A student of the California School of Fine Arts, he later

b. 1913
Banking and Law (10)

painted a mural in the San Francisco Chamber of Commerce building. He is also represented by easel works in the San Francisco Museum of Art, the Library of Congress, and the Carnegie Institute. He had a long career as professor in the Art Department at Stanford University. In his Coit Tower mural he left behind a veritable "sociogram" of his fellow artists by painting their names as "authors" of sometimes unflattering book titles like *Rape, Mayhem,* and *Married Women*. Harris at present lives in France.

W I L L I A M   H E S T H A L , another of the younger artists at Coit Tower, was born in San Francisco. He too attended the California School of Fine

b. 1908
Railroad and Shipping
(3)

Arts and has works at the San Francisco Museum of Art. In addition, he was one of six muralists whom art connoisseur Albert Bender commissioned in 1936 to decorate the Anne Bremer Library at Hesthal's alma mater, today called the San Francisco Art Institute; in two fresco lunettes he portrayed symbolic representations of the artist and society, dealing with painting in its inspired and its commercial aspects. One of Harris's "law library authors," Hesthal is credited with a book titled *Counterfeiting*. Hesthal lives in Santa Barbara, having retired from the directorship of the Santa Barbara Museum of Art.

J O H N   L A N G L E Y   H O W A R D , son of John Galen Howard and brother of sculptor Robert Howard, was born in New Jersey shortly before

b. 1902
*California Industrial
Scenes* (2)

his talented family moved west. He attended the University of California and the California School (College) of Arts and Crafts, as well as the Art Students' League of New York. One newspaper account of his large mural at Coit Tower mentioned that the painting, which depicts "the mining, hydroelectric power, and orchard industries of the State" shows an "anachronistic but forceful jumble of State activities [from] 1840 down to the present." This fresco is his only work in that medium, though he has executed many easel paintings, particularly for sports magazines, depicting fishing equipment, tools and specialized machines in meticulous detail. He lives in San Francisco.

R O B E R T   B .   H O W A R D , another son of architect John Galen Howard, came to Berkeley at age five with his family. After studying at the Col-

1896–1983
phoenix bird above
entrance, bas relief

lege of Arts and Crafts in Oakland, he won a year's scholarship to the Art Students' League in New York. To reach New York, Howard rode a motorcycle cross-country from Berkeley, his younger artist brother, Charles, astride behind him. Because his prominent father wanted him to become an artist, Robert Howard apprenticed himself to a house painter to learn to cover large areas with paint. However, most of his commissions employed his sculpturing talent. Coit Tower architect Arthur Brown, Jr., commissioned him to do the bas-relief phoenix bird (symbol of San Francisco's many "rebirths" after several widespread fires) for the exterior of the Tower a year before the PWAP established the fund for the interior art decorations. Inspired by the Rivera ceiling fresco at the San Francisco Stock Exchange Club, Howard wanted to paint a scene of the heavenly constellations on the interior ceilings of the Tower, but that theme was not deemed appropriate for the "California 1934" motifs on the walls. In addition to the many elegant decorations he did at the Stock Exchange and Club, Howard also created the popular large black sculpture piece of killer whales now at the Academy of Sciences in Golden Gate Park, representations of gas and electricity for the Pacific Gas and Electric Company, and a twenty-foot-high Buddha for the Cambodian theme of a 1930s San Francisco Artists' Parilia Ball. He also exhibited widely at local and national museums. For a time he taught sculpture at the San Francisco Art Institute. He was married to sculptor Adeline Kent. In another San Francisco fresco, Lucien Labaudt portrayed Robert Howard playing a harmonica at the apex of a human pyramid on the east wall of the Beach Chalet.

L U C I E N   L A B A U D T, after studying in England, came to the United States in 1910 from his native France. He led a rich and varied life as a costume designer for the San Francisco Artists' Parilia Balls of the 1920s and 1930s and the Bohemian High Jinx affairs, as a couturier of high fashion in San Francisco, as an easel artist experimenting with new genres, and as a frescoist of lively and popular scenes. He specifically asked to decorate the curving walls of the staircase at Coit Tower with busy, populous Powell Street, the locale of his California School of Design (now gone). In 1936 at George Washington High School in San Francisco he completed a fresco panel called *Advancement of Learning Through the Printing Press*, depicting the historical figures of science, literature, and religion who could disseminate their learning via the printed word. Another appealing fresco shows San Francisco scenes and personalities at the Beach Chalet (1936–37). In 1937 he wrote that whatever government restrictions in the art projects might *seem* to hamper the artist, "limitation forces one to think and therefore to create. . . . Far from destroying the artist's individuality, these limitations give him something to fight for. He must solve a problem." During World War II Labaudt went to India as an artist war correspondent. He was killed en route to China in an airplane crash in 1943. For many years his widow maintained the Lucien Labaudt Art Gallery in San Francisco especially for young or not widely exhibited artists.

1880–1943
Powell Street (21)

G O R D O N   L A N G D O N emerges as an almost mythical figure who came, remained briefly, and then moved on. His contemporaries remember him as "a handsome young man," affluent and urbane, a friend of Ralph Stackpole and George Harris. That he painted murals in San Francisco in the 1930s is indisputable. He has left a legacy of three frescoes: his Tower mural; *Modern and Ancient Science* over the main entrance to the library at George Washington High School; and *The Arts of Man* in the Anne Bremer Memorial Library at the San Francisco Art Institute, commissioned, along with works of five other artists (all of whom painted at Coit Tower), by Albert Bender in 1936. This allegorical lunette portrays all the various phases of printing. Stackpole wrote that Mrs. Leon Sloss commissioned Langdon to paint a fresco in her dining room as well as portraits of her three grandchildren.

ca. 1910–1960s
California Agricultural Industry (15)

J O S E   M O Y A   D E L   P I N O, an "old world" artist of great personal charm, was born in Priego, a small town in the province of Córdoba, Spain. As a boy of nine he was apprenticed to an itinerant artist who painted religious pictures of patron saints and lived by traveling from village to village selling his works to peasants and small churches. By 1907 Moya was studying at the Academy of Fine Arts in Madrid, from which he graduated with honors, winning a traveling scholarship. By 1915 he was associating with the Spanish Post-Impressionists, including Juan Gris and Diego Rivera. He painted a portrait of King Alfonso III of Spain in the early 1920s and spent four years painting forty-one reproducitons of Velasquez's paintings in El Prado, Madrid, and in Valencia. King Alfonso asked him to travel with the collection to the New World as a goodwill gesture. The exhibit ended in San Francisco, where Moya settled, depending mainly on portraiture for his livelihood. Otis Oldfield asked him to paint an oil lunette bay scene for the Coit Tower lobby in 1934. Thereafter, Moya won a competition for a mural in the Stockton, California, post office, sponsored by the PWAP. He later painted public art in Redwood City and San Rafael, in addition to a great deal of easel art. In 1928 he married artist Helen Horst; Labaudt has painted Moya del Pino holding his first-born daughter as a baby in the Powell Street staircase fresco in Coit Tower. Exhibiting widely, Moya del Pino won many awards for his esthetic and technical mastery.

1891–1969
San Francisco Bay, North (17)

O T I S   O L D F I E L D wanted to be a printer in his early days in Sacramento, California, and after a variety of manual labor jobs came to San Francisco to enroll in Arthur Best's private art school. In 1911 he went to Paris, where he remained for the next sixteen years; his subsequent San Francisco exhibit of European works had a significant impact on the local art colony. In 1924 he began teaching

1890–1969
San Francisco Bay, East (16); Seabirds and Bay Area Map (19)

at the California School of Fine Arts, and in 1925 he won the Gold Medal Award for graphic arts for his drawing *Knife Grinder*. In 1926 Oldfield married Helen Clark, a talented art student of his, in a ceremony in the stone-cutting yard behind sculptor Ralph Stackpole's studio. Thereafter the Oldfields lived on Telegraph Hill, where they maintained a studio. For the Coit Tower elevator lobby of which he was art supervisor, Oldfield painted two bird lunettes and a map as well as a harbor scene with bright boats, as viewed from his studio window. A rather short, slim man, Oldfield appears in Labaudt's Powell Street mural wearing his jaunty French beret. Throughout his career he synthesized his American and French training; in viewing the two styles, he said, "We Americans can paint circles around others in matters of feeling, but we need to learn some of the others' technical competence."

F R E D   O L M S T E D ,   J R . , grandson of Frederick Law Olmsted, the famous planner of New York's Central Park, and son of F.L. Olmsted, landscape architect and conservationist, was born in San Francisco. A painter and sculptor and later an architect, twenty-three-year-old Fred Olmsted initially came onto the Tower project to assist John Langley Howard and George Harris. Howard later assigned him the three-foot panel above the main entrance; in it Olmsted created *Power*, a fist bursting through a lightning jag. Modestly, he hid his signature so that the viewer can see it only by standing on tiptoe, in just the right light. He was one of six Tower artists whom Albert Bender selected for decorating the Anne Bremer Memorial Library at the San Francisco Art Institue. A critic in 1936 said of his lunette there that it was "one of the most colorful of the whole series, folk art represented in the work of the American Indian potter." Later he created murals in the Utah State Capitol. Now gone is a mural for the library of the San Francisco Boys' Club showing a closely packed Rivera-style scene of active boys. Students at City College of San Francisco remember Olmsted for his two large heads of tufa stone: Thomas Edison and Leonardo da Vinci (1941—WPA) outside the east entrance of Timothy Pfleuger's science building. Inside the main entrance he painted two fresco panels showing students engaged in various scientific pursuits in a semi-abstract composition (1942—WPA).

b. 1911
Power (20)

S U Z A N N E   S C H E U E R chose to work on the complex process of newspaper production in her panel at Coit Tower. With assistant Hebe Daum, Scheuer brightened her corner of the Tower with more blues and reds than the usual earth tones of the fresco palette. Later she painted murals in two Texas post offices, at Caldwell and Eastland. Her work also adorns a wall in the Berkeley, California, post office. At present she is living in retirement in Santa Cruz, California.

b. 1898
Newsgathering (6)

R A L P H S T A C K P O L E grew up in Oregon, coming to San Francisco after the turn of the century. "His writing is lucid and excellent, perhaps because he barely finished the eighth grade in a backwoods Oregon school," said one of his prize students, Fred Olmsted. He worked with sculptor Arthur Putnam and painter Gottardo Piazzoni, then went to Paris to study at the Ecole des Beaux Arts. Upon his return to San Francisco he became part of the art scene of the teens and twenties. Remarked Olmsted, "Stackpole stretches over two generations. While I was first chewing a rubber ring he was well established making sensitive and illustrative portraits—children, friends, famous people." He went on to wonder how Stackpole could create, faced as he was "with the necessities of both constant innovation and monumental work," yet "his work stands all over the state, the chips forming a geological layercake on the stoneyard floor." As early as 1919 Stackpole was creating bronze heads, e.g., James Seawell, in City Hall. Timothy Pfleuger commissioned two carved pylons representing *Earth's Fruitfulness* and *Man's Inventive Genius* in 1931–32 to stand outside the San Francisco Stock Exchange. It was Stackpole who knew Edward Bruce and suggested telegraphing him when Zakheim proposed that the artists organize in 1933.

1885–1973
Industries of California
(5)

After Coit Tower, Stackpole went to work on frescoes at George Washington High School (*Contemporary Education*) and at the San Francisco Art Institute's Anne Bremer Library (*Architecture and Sculpture*). At the time of the Coit Tower lockout, Stackpole wrote that he wanted to see frescoes "spread all over the city; San Francisco would even be called the City of Frescoes as Portland is called the City of Roses. But it strikes me that those Coit Tower frescoes are shut up in a tomb." A friend of many artists, Stackpole appears in both Albro's and Zakheim's murals.

E D W A R D T E R A D A came to San Francisco from Japan to study at the California School of Fine Arts with Otis Oldfield and later returned to study with Sekido Yoshida in Japan. At the Tower he painted a scene of sports activities, featuring an enlarged "Persian miniature" of polo players on horseback. He is an artist in many genres—a painter of portraits and miniatures, a sculptor, a block printer, a general designer, a draftsman, a lithographer, an etcher, and a good teacher. After World War II Terada went to live in Japan where he continues to work.

b. 1908
Sports (23)

F R E D E V I D A R , born in Denmark, came to San Francisco as a high-school student with his parents. He began painting at age twelve, studying at the School of Fine Arts for six years after graduating from the High School of Commerce. He studied with Matisse and Dufy in Paris for a short period in 1933, returning in time to join the Coit Tower project in 1934. At twenty-four he won a prestigious prize

b. 1911
Department Store (11)

to study art for three years in Paris. He spoke of his painting as "largely an emotional matter, not a studied and carefully calculated thing," though a local critic said that he was "the finest draftsman this town has had in recent years." He preferred painting cities and people to flowers or still life. "The fun comes in organizing the life around one in artistic form, adjusting the world to a space and a medium." Another critic wrote during a Los Angeles exhibit in 1941 that though Vidar "is a sure draftsman and knows how to make color perform," the American Allegory paintings that he displayed were "surrealistic jumbles" that never attained that "unity of his 'straight' figure or landscape pieces." In the "law library," Harris painted his name as Herr Vidar, "author" of Laws on Seduction.

C L I F F O R D   W I G H T, like Gordon Langdon, came, created, and departed without biographical traces. That he left his mark cannot be denied,

ca. 1900–1960s
Surveyor and
Steelworker (4); Farmer
and Cowboy (12)

for it was on his Communist logo that the controversy centered, keeping the doors to Coit Tower locked during the summer of 1934. In a book on Diego Rivera, Bertram Wolfe spoke of Wight as "an English sculptor" who assisted Rivera first in Detroit and then on the Rockefeller Center fresco in New York, destroyed in 1933 because it contained a portrait of Lenin. The San Francisco Art Commission said that Wight was resorting to a Rivera-style publicity stunt by using the hammer-and-sickle symbol at Coit Tower, but Wight protested that it represented just one of several alternative economic systems of the times. He denied being a Communist, saying to the Art Commission when it demanded that he obliterate the "offensive" portion of his fresco "I merely exercised my right of free expression. It was just a symbol—not propaganda. I object to my work being erased." Several artists have recognized Wight's Coit Tower Cowboy as a self-portrait.

B E R N A R D   B A R U C H   Z A K H E I M arrived in San Francisco in 1920 seeking political asylum, as he could not return to his native Poland

b. 1896
Library (7)

after World War I. An upholsterer by trade, he had begun art studies in Europe and continued them at the Mark Hopkins Art Institute (later called the California School of Fine Arts, and today, the San Francisco Art Institute). Having won by competition the first fresco project in a building with public access in San Francisco, the Jewish Community Center, he, together with Ralph Stackpole, had the prestige necessary to organize the artists to ask for a federally sponsored art project. Although he would rather have painted the street scene at the Tower, he was able to make the "innocuous" library a vehicle for the message that he wanted to communicate. On Harris's "authors" list, he is credited with Married Women.

After Coit Tower, he portrayed Community Spirit for the Alemany Health Center (1934), and then undertook the four-year task of illustrating the history of medicine at the University of California Medical Center (1935–38). In 1938 he painted oil murals for post offices in Texas. In 1961 Zakheim returned to Poland to do a 6- by 25-foot fresco called *The History of the Jews Through Song.* In recent years he has been sculpturing in wood and granite in his Sebastopol, California, orchard. Continuing the themes of human suffering and protest that have long motivated him, he carved six large figures in wood on the subject of the Holocaust, called *Genocide* (1966). About working with wood Zakheim has written: "With chisel the artist unveils the beautiful calligraphy nature has embedded like grain in the wood. . . . The Sculptor's blood from wounds gives life to the wood."

NOTES

The Construction of the Tower

1. Hittell, J. *History of California*, Vol. III, p. 349
2. *Ibid.*
3. Holdredge, Helen. *Firebelle Lillie*, p. 247
4. Park Commission minutes, 1931; Recreation and Park Department, San Francisco
5. Atherton, Gertrude. *My San Francisco: A Wayward Biography*, p. 30
6. Park Commission minutes, *op. cit.*, 12/17/31
7. *Ibid.*, p. 85
8. San Francisco *Chronicle*, 11/2/52 (California Historical Society Archives)
9. Gilliam, Harold. *The San Francisco Experience*, p. 17
10. Howard, Henry T. "The Coit Memorial Tower," *Architect and Engineer*, 115:3, p. 11
11. *Ibid.*, p. 13
12. *Ibid.*, p. 15
13. Whittick, Arnold. *European Architecture in the Twentieth Century*, p. 234
14. Williams, I.T., and H.M. Palmer. *Dictionary of National Biography*, p. 871
15. In Egyptian mythology, the phoenix was a beautiful, lone bird which lived in the Arabian desert for five hundred to six hundred years and then consumed itself in fire, rising renewed from the ashes to start another long life; hence it is a symbol of immortality *(Webster's College Dictionary)*. After the great fire of 1906, stage designer and illustrator Albertine Randall Wheelan designed the San Francisco Public Library bookplate showing the phoenix rising from the flames. Its motto, *"Vita sine literis mors est,"* translates, "Life without literature is death." (Vol. I, p. 65, San Francisco Library Art Clippings, Art Department)

New Deal Support for the Arts

1. McKinzie, Richard D. *The New Deal for Artists*, p. 4
2. The WPA defended their support as follows: "[The purposes of the FAP-WPA are mainly to] take talented artists off the relief roles . . . to advance art as a definite asset to the State . . . and to produce for the State works of permanent value." (WPA Bulletin, 1936)
3. Letter from Vernon C. Porter to Charles Sheeler, 12/30/33
4. Watson, Forbes. "New Forces in American Art" (condensed from the *Kenyon Review*, Vol. I, No. 2), p. 12
5. McKinzie, Richard D., *op cit.*, p. 59
6. Bruce to Heil, telegram dated 12/10/33
7. Minutes of the Second Meeting of the Regional Committee, District 15, PWAP, 12/18/33

8. Condensed by MZJ from an interview with Bernard B. Zakheim by Lewis Ferbraché, Archives of American Art, Smithsonian Institution, San Francisco, 1964

The Story of the Murals

1. Letter from Dr. Walter Heil to Edward Rowan; emphasis added by MZJ
2. Interview with Bernard B. Zakheim by Lewis Ferbraché, condensed by MZJ, Archives of American Art, Smithsonian Institution, San Francisco, 1964
3. Oral interview of Mrs. Otis Oldfield by MZJ
4. Lavrova, Nadia. "Forty-six Artists and One Palette," *Christian Science Monitor*, 8/8/34
5. It is a nostalgic myth in artistic circles that Matthew Barnes, a plasterer and beloved local artist, applied the thin surface coat of fresco plaster each dawn for the day's work. Actually, he did not work at Coit Tower, calling the quality of artwork at the Tower "so much tripe," according to one artist. The two plasterers hired on the grant were Joseph Kelly and William Simpson. Heil's records do show, however, that Matthew Barnes received $42.50 as a "mural coordinator."
6. Heil Papers; AAA, NDA 3, Fr. 715–31
7. Bruce, Edward. "Implications of the PWAP," *American Magazine of Art*, March 1934

Politics, Sensationalism, and the Murals

1. San Francisco *Chronicle*, 1/11/34, p. 10, col. 2
2. Letter from Forbes Watson to Dr. Walter Heil, 1/29/34
3. San Francisco *News*, 6/23/34
4. San Francisco *News*, 2/14/34
5. *Ibid.*
6. Camp, William. *San Francisco Port of Gold*, p. 437; quoted by Fr. John McGloin in *San Francisco: The Story of a City*, p. 313
7. Hailey, Gene, ed. *California Art Research Project*, First Series, WPA Proj. 2874, Vol. XX, p.64
8. Cravens, Junius, quoted by Gene Hailey, *op. cit.*
9. *Ibid.*, p. 71
10. McKinzie, Richard D. *The New Deal for Artists*, p. 25
11. McGloin, *op. cit.*, p. 316
12. Telegram, Heil to Watson, 6/2/34
13. McKinzie, *op. cit.*, pp 24–5
14. Seely, Evelyn. "A Frescoed Tower Clangs Shut Amid Gasps," *Literary Digest*, 8/25/34, p. 244
15. San Francisco *Examiner*, 7/5/34
16. Hailey, *op cit.*, p. 64
17. McGloin, *op. cit.*, p. 316
18. Wight, Clifford. "Statement to Dr. Heil and the San Francisco Art Commission," unpublished, undated
19. McKinzie, *op. cit.*, p. 25
20. Letter from Mr. Harlan to Edward Bruce, 7/20/34
21. Hailey, *op. cit.*, p. 70
22. Cravens, Junius. "City May Be Proud of Mural Decorations Put on Coit Tower," San Francisco *News*, 10/20/34

A Historical Overview

1. San Francisco *Examiner* editorial, 7/9/34
2. San Francisco *Chronicle*, 8/26/53, p. 15
3. Adams, Ben. *San Francisco: An Informal Guide*, p. 141
4. Seeley, Evelyn. "A Frescoed Tower Clangs Shut Amid Gasps," *Literary Digest*, 8/25/34
5. Gelber, Steven. "San Francisco's 'Commie' Art," *City of San Francisco* magazine, Vol. 10, No. 30, 2/4/76, p. 37

BIBLIOGRAPHY

Adams, Ben. *San Francisco: An Informal Guide*. New York: Hill and Wang, 1968

Archives of American Art, Smithsonian Institution, San Francisco Branch

Archives of American Art, Smithsonian Institution, Washington Branch

Atherton, Gertrude. *My San Francisco: A Wayward Biography*. Indianapolis: Bobbs Merrill, 1946

Bowlen, Frederick J. *Lilly Hitchcock Coit*. San Francisco, 1937 (at Coit Tower)

Bruce, Edward. "Implications of the Public Works of Art Projects," *American Magazine of Art*, March 1934

Gelber, Steven. "San Francisco's 'Commie' Art," *City of San Francisco* magazine, Vol. 10, No. 30, February 4, 1976

Gilliam, Harold. *The San Francisco Experience*. New York: Doubleday, 1972

Hailey, Gene, ed. *California Art Research Project*, First Series, WPA Project, 2874, Vol. XX

Heil, Dr. Walter. *Papers*. Archives of American Art, NDA 3, Fr. 715–31, Art. Smithsonian Institution, San Francisco, 1964

Hittell, T. *History of California*, Vol. III, San Francisco, 1897

Holdredge, Helen. *Firebelle Lillie*. New York: Meredith Press, 1967

Howard, Henry T. "The Coit Memorial Tower," *Architect and Engineer*, 115, No. 3, December 1933, 11–15

Jewett, Masha Zakheim. "A Guide to the Coit Tower Murals," *California Living* magazine, San Francisco *Examiner*, December 14, 1975

Lavrova, Nadia. "Forty-six Artists and One Palette," *Christian Science Monitor*, August 8, 1934

Maleville, Michelle. "Historic American Building Survey: Coit Tower." Davis: University of California, 1968 (unpub. ms.)

McGloin, Fr. John. *San Francisco: The Story of a City*. San Rafael: Presidio Press, 1978

McKinzie, Richard D. *The New Deal for Artists*. Princeton: Princeton University Press, 1973

Minutes of the Second Meeting of the Regional Committee, District 15, Public Works of Art, December 18, 1933

Myrick, David. *Telegraph Hill*. Berkeley: Howell-North Books, 1972

O'Connor, Francis V. "A Sampler of New Deal Murals," *American Heritage*, October 1970

San Francisco Public Library Art Department. Art Clippings, Vol. I, 65

San Francisco Recreation and Park Department minutes, 1931, 1932, 1933

Seeley, Evelyn. "A Frescoed Tower Clangs Shut Amid Gasps," *Literary Digest*, August 25, 1934

Summary of *The History of Coit Tower* (San Francisco Recreation and Park Department minutes), San Francisco, undated (unpub. ms.)

Watson, Forbes. "New Forces in American Art" (condensed from the
    Kenyon Review, Vol. I, No. 2), 1936
Whittick, Arnold. *European Architecture in the Twentieth Century.*
    Aylesbury, Bucks.: International Textbook Company, 1974
Williams, I.T., and H.M. Palmer. *Dictionary of National Biography, 1951
    –60,* London: Oxford University Press, 1971

Newspaper Articles

Christian Science Monitor: Lavrova, Nadia. "Forty-six Artists and One
    Palette." Weekly magazine section, August 8, 1934
San Francisco *Chronicle:* January 11, 1934; November 2, 1952; August
    26, 1953; October 21, 1957; November 19, 1957
San Francisco *Examiner:* July 5, 1934; editorial, July 9, 1934
San Francisco *News:* February 14, 1934; June 23, 1934; July 10, 1934

Letters

Archives of Public Works of Art, 1933–34
Mr. Harlan to Edward Bruce, July 20, 1934
Vernon C. Porter to Charles Sheeler, December 30, 1933
Forbes Watson to Dr. Walter Heil, January 29, 1934

Oral Interviews by Masha Zakheim Jewett

Ralph Chesse
Edith Hamlin
William Hesthal
John Langley Howard
Robert Howard
Marcelle Labaudt
Helen Oldfield
Bernard Zakheim

Telegrams

Dr. Walter Heil to Forbes Watson, December 10, 1933, and June 2, 1934
    (Public Works of Art Project, Archives of American Art)